THE FREEDOM MANIFESTO

THE FREEDOM MANIFESTO

MARÍA CORINA MACHADO
NOBEL PEACE PRIZE LAUREATE

Regnery books may be purchased in bulk at special discounts for sales promotion, corporate gifts, fund-raising, or educational purposes. Special editions can also be created to specifications. For details, contact the Special Sales Department, Regnery, 307 Fifth Avenue, 4th Floor, New York, NY 10016 or info@skyhorsepublishing.com.

Regnery® is an imprint of Skyhorse Publishing, Inc.®, a Delaware corporation.

Visit our website at www.regnery.com.
Please follow our publisher Tony Lyons on Instagram @tonylyonsisuncertain.

10 9 8 7 6 5 4 3 2 1

Library of Congress Cataloging-in-Publication Data is available on file.

Cover design by Brian Peterson

Hardcover ISBN: 978-1-5107-8777-3
Paperback ISBN: 978-1-5107-8749-0
Ebook ISBN: 978-1-5107-8754-4

Printed in the United States of America

*To all who cherish freedom enough to stand for it,
no matter the risk.*

All proceeds from the sale of this publication will support the initiatives of The María Corina Machado Foundation for Freedom and Democracy, dedicated to advancing democratic restoration, safeguarding human rights, and fostering individual development.

CONTENTS

A TIMELINE OF MODERN VENEZUELAN HISTORY

Venezuela's Democratic Period (1958–1999)—and the Seeds of Collapse

- **1958.** Venezuela holds its first free elections, ushering in a "democratic era," marked by regular elections, peaceful transfers of power, civil liberties, and oil-fueled growth.
- **1976.** The state nationalizes the oil industry and is increasingly seen as a provider and protector. Wealth grows while accountability erodes.
- **1992.** Two failed military coups, on February 4 and November 27 (the first one led by Hugo Chávez).

The Chávez "Revolution" (1999–2012): Authoritarian Backsliding

- **1998.** Hugo Chávez wins Venezuela's presidential election.
- **1999.** The Constituent Assembly produces a new Constitution that eliminates the Senate, introduces reelection, and concentrates power in the president. Democratic fragility gives way to authoritarian design.

- **1999–2004**. Judicial takeover: massive purge of judges and temporary appointments.
- **2003.** State-owned oil industry (PDVSA) workers hold a general strike. Half of the industry's oil workers (twenty thousand) are fired, and Chávez takes direct control of the industry.
- **2007. Student movement emerges:** Mass university protests erupt nationwide following the shutdown of a TV station critical of Chávez, defending freedom of expression and marking the birth of a new civic opposition generation.
- **2013.** Chávez names Nicolás Maduro his successor. Oil prices remain high—a financial windfall that helps underwrite the government's political projects even after his death later that year.

The Maduro Era (2013–2025): Fraud, Violence, Poverty, Exodus, and Authoritarianism

- **2013.** Following Chávez's death, Maduro comes to power in an election rife with fraud.
- **2014, 2017.** Two large protest cycles are violently repressed. Over twenty thousand detentions; massive human rights violations.
- State-criminal symbiosis with transnational branches. Tens of thousands of extrajudicial executions.
- **2014.** Beginning of the mass exodus. Venezuelans begin migrating in large numbers amid economic collapse, widespread shortages, rising insecurity, and political persecution. The number will reach eight million by 2025.

- **2013–2021.** The largest and deepest hyperinflation cycle in the continent's history. GDP contracts 80 percent, and 30 percent of the population flees the country.

Key Dates in María Corina Machado's Fight for Venezuelan Freedom

- **2002.** Civil society reaction against an abusive Enabling Law. María Corina Machado helps to found Súmate, an electoral watch NGO.
- **2003–2004.** The Recall Referendum Drive. The constitution's recall mechanism becomes the central peaceful tool. A referendum can be triggered after half a term with signatures from 20 percent of registered voters. Súmate organizes the signature collection that makes the 2004 referendum possible. The referendum ends in massive fraud.
- **January 2010.** After a fellowship at Yale, MCM returns to Venezuela to launch a new political path.
- **2010.** MCM is elected as the most voted representative in the country (235,259 votes) in the legislative elections.
- **2012.** MCM runs in the opposition primary.
- **2014.** MCM participates in the popular protests. She is banned from leaving the country and expelled from the National Assembly. The travel ban is effective to this day.
- **2015.** MCM helps to design and implement the strategy that leads the opposition coalition to win two-thirds of the seats in the National Assembly.
- **2012–2016.** MCM founds, structures, and consolidates Vente Venezuela, a movement-party rooted in citizens and ideas rather than patronage.

- **2017.** MCM again participates in the protests and leads the citizens' massive reaction against a fraudulent Constitutional Assembly convoked by Maduro.
- **2018–2019.** MCM denounces the fraud in the presidential election and supports the National Assembly's interim government but refuses to integrate it.
- **October 22, 2023.** Opposition primary. Turnout overwhelms logistics; ballots run out. MCM wins with 92.3 percent of the vote.
- **January 26, 2024.** Venezuela's Supreme Tribunal of Justice upholds a ban preventing MCM from holding public office and barred her presidential candidacy for the 2024 election, confirming her disqualification from running despite her primary victory.
- **March 5, 2024.** The Maduro regime announces presidential elections are to be held on July 28 of that year, even though elections are traditionally held in December.
- **March 20, 2024.** Following arrest warrants issued against senior members of María Corina's presidential campaign, several members of her core team—including her campaign manager—enter the Argentine Embassy in Caracas to seek protection from detention. Venezuelan security forces maintain a constant presence outside the compound. The group remains inside under asylum conditions for more than four hundred days.
- **April 19, 2024.** The opposition coalition formally confirms Edmundo González Urrutia as its presidential candidate for the July 28 election, replacing MCM following her disqualification.

- **July 25, 2024.** Final campaign rally. Nearly two hundred thousand people gather in San Cristóbal, the largest public gathering in the city's history.
- **July 28, 2024.** Election Day. The strategy centers on securing *actas* (official machine-printed tally sheets) through *testigos* (witnesses entitled to copies). Turnout is massive despite coercion linked to food benefits. Early results appear consistent nationwide (nearly 70–30), then access is blocked and witnesses expelled. Citizens conceal and transport *actas*; clandestine teams scan and upload them. Opposition claims 85 percent of *actas* published, showing 7M+ votes for González. The regime announces results without publishing detailed tallies. In the aftermath, those linked to *actas* are hunted; detentions, disappearances, and torture are described as part of the aftermath.
- **July 29, 2024.** MCM goes into hiding, living in strict self-confinement for sixteen months, except for making appearances in five protests.
- **October 10, 2025.** MCM is announced as the recipient of the 2025 Nobel Peace Prize, in recognition of her steadfast, peaceful struggle for democratic freedom in Venezuela.
- **December 11, 2025.** MCM arrives in Oslo after leaving Venezuela in secret to collect the Nobel Prize on behalf of the people of Venezuela.

PREFACE
A SPIRITUAL AND EXISTENTIAL STRUGGLE

The Fragility of Freedom

All my life, I have heard the same words, over and over again: "It is impossible."

What you are saying is impossible.

What you are proposing is impossible.

What you are attempting is impossible.

It was impossible, people said, for someone born into a family with resources to be accepted—much less loved—by the poorest, humblest people in the country. And yet I found a home among them. They trusted me. We stood together.

It was impossible to gather three million signatures for a recall petition—until we did just that, forcing an unprecedented recall referendum against Hugo Chávez in 2004.

It was impossible for someone who is not a socialist, who has spent her life resisting socialism, to be embraced by a nation that has known nothing else.

It was impossible, in a country as deeply *machista* as Venezuela, for a woman to become a national leader.

And it was impossible to fight for—and win—freedom in a nation that, for the past twenty-six years, had lived under the dominance of the state: dependence, corruption, violence, terror, and the endless pleading for rights that should have been ours all along.

It was impossible. All of it.

So we—the people of Venezuela—made it possible.

*

I belong to a generation of Venezuelans who took freedom for granted.

During the democratic era of our history, which lasted from 1958 to 1999, we held regular elections, witnessed peaceful transfers of power, protected civil liberties, and enjoyed periods of remarkable economic growth. Blessed with oil, Venezuela possessed so much abundance that wealth was often treated as limitless. Over time, many came to believe that by virtue of being Venezuelan, they were entitled to a share of it. Venezuelans of my generation grew up believing our country would always be prosperous, secure, and free.

From this belief, two insidious ideas took root. The first was that the state—rich, powerful, and permanent—could manage your life, provide for your needs, and shield you from hardship. The second was that it would grant you rights and require nothing in exchange.

But nothing is free. Nothing. You must always give something away. What people of my generation and those who came before us did not understand—until it was too late—was precisely what we were giving away: our power to decide.

A society that does not demand accountability; that does not prize transparency, merit, and the honest reward of effort; and that does not organize on its own behalf invites privilege to decay into corruption. Dependence deepens into poverty.

That's what happened in Venezuela over the course of my lifetime. It is what prepared the ground for dictators like Hugo Chávez and Nicolás Maduro to take control—men who framed revenge and resentment as justice and promised enforced equality as the redress of perceived grievances. All at the expense of democracy, individual liberty, and the Venezuelan people's right to decide their own future.

We failed to understand something that we have since learned with absolute and painful clarity: freedom comes with responsibility. Freedom requires participation. And freedom is never free.

Everyone must do their part. There is a cost, and we all must share it.

*

By the time Chávez took power in 1999, we had already lost sight of how fragile our freedom was. Venezuela became like the proverbial frog in a pot of slowly heating water. At first, many did not realize just how much was at stake.

The regime would make it clear.

Chávez began by focusing on controlling the judicial system. He understood that law and justice are the pillars on which every other part of society rests. Within just a few years, he had purged more than 90 percent of the country's sitting judges. Anyone who was not absolutely loyal was expelled and replaced. There is nothing resembling an independent judiciary in Venezuela.

An estimated 97 percent of judges hold temporary appointments—positions they can lose overnight if they fail to demonstrate complete fealty to the regime.

Over the past two decades, there has not been a single case in which a jury or judge has ruled in favor of an individual against the state. No one would ever dare. To do so would mean prison—or worse.

Next, he trained his sights on the oil.

Before Chávez, PDVSA, Venezuela's state-owned oil company, operated with a degree of independence. Its revenues were unevenly managed, and corruption certainly existed, but the company had not been weaponized into an instrument of political control.

Chávez saw enormous potential and seized the opportunity.

Using a national strike in 2003 as a pretext for swift punishment, he fired over twenty thousand people in a single stroke and took control of the company. More than half of its workforce was expelled—from the president of the corporation to the engineers and technicians who kept it running. One of the largest oil companies in the world was suddenly placed in the hands of a dictator and his military, transformed into a fully subordinated political instrument and a source of unimaginable personal wealth.

When Chávez took office, oil prices hovered around eight dollars a barrel. In less than a decade, they surpassed one hundred. Before his death in 2013, prices reached as high as $147. The amount of money that flowed through his hands in those years is almost beyond comprehension—more than the Venezuelan state had received over its entire century as an oil-producing nation.

In capturing the judiciary and seizing the nation's resources, he was determined to make Venezuelan society absolutely dependent on him, and on him alone. He became the state. To deepen that dependence, he took over private companies and productive industries at will. Entrepreneurs and business owners lost everything. He then turned against the financial sector and against any part of the economy that might serve as a source of resistance.

And still, it was not enough. Chávez next set out to systematically destroy the value of the national currency, the bolívar, intentionally impoverishing the population while consolidating control over vast natural resources and his ever-expanding personal power.

It was cruel, but also strategic. The objective was simple: to ensure that people had no choice but to rely exclusively on the regime for survival.

As salaries collapsed and savings evaporated, the regime introduced the idea of a monthly "bonus"—a lifeline granted by the state, but only to those who behaved. If you did not behave, you could still receive your salary—sometimes the equivalent of a single dollar a day—but you would not receive the bonus.

To "take care of the poor," the regime created a program called the Local Committees for Supply and Production (CLAP). These committees delivered boxes of food to millions of newly desperate households. And like the bonuses, the boxes were contingent on good behavior. It was not a right, but a reward—for obedience to whatever the regime demanded.

To enforce compliance, local street chiefs were appointed to act as political agents. In this way, they built a structure that was both wide and deep, penetrating every neighborhood, every block, and every household.

They went street by street, entering people's names into a vast database called Sistema Patria. They recorded everything about everyone—where you worked, what you bought, how you voted, who your relatives were. Benefits were distributed according to your loyalty. Or they were withheld.

With the assistance of the Cuban regime, which helped design and manage much of this system, and China, which provided key technology, the state was able to penetrate nearly every dimension of Venezuelan life.

It did not take long for Chávez to transform Venezuela into an impoverished society—living in fear, its head bowed, and its hands extended. If you failed to do as they demanded, dress as they wanted, or gather when ordered to gather, you would not receive food. And you would not receive the gas to cook it with.

But private humiliations were not enough. It was also important to punish publicly.

Whenever possible, the regime made a point of spotlighting exemplary cases of people who ran afoul of the state—another practice they learned from the Cuban regime.

One such example was made of Judge María Lourdes Afiuni. She refused to comply with a direct order from Chávez and instead issued a lawful ruling in a politically sensitive case. For that single act of independence, Chávez ordered her arrest. She was imprisoned for more than three and a half years, much of it in a tiny cell without sunlight, and later held under armed house arrest. During her detention, she was raped, abused, and humiliated. She was dismissed from her position, her family was persecuted, and she remains under restrictive measures to this day, effectively barred from work and from leaving the country.

Her case was meant to show every other judge what happens

when you fall out of line. The regime repeated this tactic across every sector of society until no man, woman, or child was left untouched by their tyranny and control.

With journalists, the approach was especially methodical. At first, it was quiet—restrictions placed on media outlets the regime didn't trust, money funneled to others willing to reproduce the official narrative. But before long, the threats became explicit. One by one, the largest media organizations were forced to close—or submit to the regime. The approach was remarkably effective. Today, most journalists have left the country. Yet even from abroad, many are still afraid to speak. They have a cousin, a parent, a grandmother still living in Venezuela—and in recent months, the regime has intensified its brutality against the family members of those who speak out. Journalists continue to be detained arbitrarily for doing their work. Some have spent years in prison without due process, simply for telling the truth.

With the military, the regime was equally deliberate—and equally cruel.

Chávez came from the armed forces. He understood that a professional military would never accept Venezuela's sovereignty being handed over to foreign powers such as Cuba, Russia, Iran, or China. He knew the institution would have to be destroyed from within. From the moment he took power, the military ceased to function as a meritocracy. The best officers no longer advanced. Instead, promotions flowed downward—to those whose sole qualification was unconditional loyalty to the regime.

Once those individuals were securely in the regime's grip, Chávez went about dismantling their livelihoods and their moral integrity. Legitimate sources of income were destroyed while corruption and narco-trafficking were deliberately encouraged. If you wanted to feed your family, you looked to illegal activities, further binding you to the crimes of the state against the people.

Repression became the military's primary objective. The Bolivarian National Guard, in particular, was deployed as the regime's main instrument against civilian protest. In 2014 and again in 2017, widespread antiregime demonstrations erupted across Venezuela, stretching over months and accounting for dozens of deaths. Countless young Venezuelans were injured, arrested, or imprisoned as security forces cracked down on dissent. I think of David José Vallenilla, a twenty-two-year-old student shot and killed at close range in broad daylight by a military official in Caracas as he was bringing medical supplies to protesters. His murder was caught on camera for the world to see. I think of Juan Pablo Pernalete, twenty years old, whose mother begged him not to go out that day—she still remembers him saying, “Mom, protesting is not a crime; protesting means that things are not right.” He was killed by a tear gas canister fired by a National Guardsman. Nine years later, his mother, Elvira, and his father, José Gregorio, still keep his room intact—his basketball uniform folded, his trophies in place. Despite their deep grief, they have inspired hundreds of victims' families to demand justice. Their courage renews my own resolve to fight for the country that all these young lives cut short deserved to inherit.

Repression extended inward to soldiers themselves and their families. Any soldier who chose to honor their oath instead of obeying abusive orders was labeled a “traitor” and lost not only their freedom, but also their home on the military base, their income, and their access to hospitals and schools. By using the families as leverage, essentially holding them hostage, the regime ensured silence, obedience, and fear throughout the ranks. Acts of cruelty toward soldiers are carried out in full view. I think of Captain Rafael Acosta Arévalo, who was detained, tortured so brutally that he could not stand at his own hearing, and brought before a military court barely able to speak before he died from his injuries. His death sent a message to every officer in uniform: dissent would be crushed without mercy.

To their great credit, the universities resisted the regime for a very long time. In the past, when protests erupted, we would run into the universities for protection. That safety is gone. Even private universities—once safe spaces where our young people could speak freely—have been compromised by the regime. Presidents have been dismissed. Professors have been imprisoned for publishing statistics that the regime deemed inconvenient. New authorities have been installed, chosen solely for their unconditional loyalty.

Yet throughout this era of repression, university students have remained a persistent source of resistance and civic courage. A national student movement emerged in the mid-2000s as part of wider opposition to closures of independent media and constitutional overreach, and it has continued to lead demonstrations against corruption, insecurity, and repression since, inspiring citizens across generations, at great personal cost. Many, many students have been jailed and killed over the years. They have been the heartbeat of dissent in our nation.

The Venezuelan Catholic Church remained one of the most

powerful forces in our society. After all, more than 90 percent of our population is Christian. Yet even this institution was not spared from attempts to terrorize it into silence.

The regime began withholding government funds that had long supported Church-run education and social programs. At the same time, it targeted specific priests and bishops for persecution. The message was unmistakable—speak out, and your parish, your school, your community will pay the price.

Although a very few members of the Church have succumbed to regime pressures, most bishops and priests in Venezuela have shown extraordinary courage. They continued to protect the persecuted and to offer refuge, often quietly and without recognition, even as regime-aligned forces sought to discredit them and public campaigns aimed to destroy their reputations.

*

The regime's brutality did not stop at institutions. It reached deep into the lives of individual citizens. This was more than authoritarianism; it was totalitarianism. They wanted control over the body and the mind. And not only control, but total domination.

Years ago, a good friend of mine, Fernando Anzola, owned agricultural land in the state of Lara, one of Venezuela's most important farming regions. He was productive, independent, and deeply rooted in his community. One day, while he was at home with his six-year-old daughter and his wife, who was pregnant at the time, a regime agent appeared at their door. He came with a simple order: Fernando had to leave immediately. The state was taking over.

"But this is our home," Fernando said. "We have worked this land for decades. Everything we have is here."

"You have to go," came the reply.

In a matter of hours, the family lost their home. Terrified, Fernando's wife lost her baby. The state seized the *finca*—not to develop it, not to redistribute it, but to destroy it. Today, the land lies idle. It produces nothing.

This kind of terror was being unleashed all across the country. It still is.

Just a few months ago, the regime went looking for a member of our party, Miguel, who had once helped provide security as we traveled around the country. When they went to his house, he wasn't there. He was in hiding.

So they took his mother and his son instead. When his daughter went to ask for them—bringing her two-year-old baby with—they detained her as well, along with the child, simply to force Miguel to come out of hiding and surrender himself.

One might think they would try to hide these abuses. But they don't. They want them to be seen.

The purpose, as always, is pure terror. They want to demonstrate—very publicly—what they are capable of doing and to instill fear in any Venezuelan who believes they cannot, or will not, come for them next.

But perhaps the regime's most effective tool has been division.

The regime understood that to maintain control, it would have to tear families apart and turn society against itself. Black against white. Rich against poor. Those who left against those who stayed. Wherever a fault line existed, they widened it. Wherever a division could be exploited, it was exploited.

This is how they came to understand the power of migration. By forcing people out of the country—as it has done with more than eight million Venezuelans—the regime produced several effects at once.

One was the release of internal pressure. Fewer people remained to demand food, electricity, and medicine. Fewer voices were capable of challenging the regime.

Another was the fracturing and scattering of families. In Venezuelan culture, the family is a protective shield—the very nucleus of our society. Women, and mothers in particular, hold enormous power.

As I traveled throughout the country, I saw the human cost everywhere. Countless children had been left alone in their homes. Their mothers were gone; their fathers had never been there. Sometimes a thirteen-year-old was raising his or her younger siblings. Anyone who could leave had gone in search of food or money to send back. Some parents would leave alone at first, to find work and stability and then, months or even years later, find a way to bring their children out of that hardship to join them.

Grandparents would approach me in tears, saying, "I don't want to die before I meet my grandchildren."

The final consequence extended beyond Venezuela's borders. The millions who fled were driven to seek refuge in neighboring countries and beyond, burdening schools, hospitals, labor markets, and social services in communities that opened their doors in good faith. What began as a domestic strategy of control became a regional humanitarian crisis, deliberately imposed on others and weaponized by the regime.

In some cases, that destabilization took on a criminal form. Groups born in Venezuela's prisons began preying on those forced to flee and exporting violence beyond our borders—turning displacement into a source of fear and insecurity across the hemisphere.

And for many Venezuelans, escape itself was a nightmare. Hundreds of thousands crossed the Darién jungle—on foot, through mud, rivers—simply to find a place where they could live. Many never made it. Others survived, carrying scars that will never heal.

All of this was intentional.

All of it was by design.

And all of it was a cruel, tragic waste of human spirit. All of it.

Reclaiming Our Destiny

I grew up on my grandmother's lap, listening to her stories. Like the story of her youngest brother, Armando, whom she adored, and who had been killed at the age of twenty-four fighting against an earlier dictator, Juan Vicente Gómez. He had given his life for freedom and for Venezuela, she said. His presence felt close and dear to me; he became, in many ways, the great inspiration of my life.

I have always felt fortunate for the family I was born into, not only because of the opportunities I had—education, material security, protection—but also because of the love and example that surrounded me from the very beginning of my life. My grandmother—and later, my father—instilled in me a sense of the great responsibility we bear for our country and for other nations as well. During the War of Independence, nearly 30 percent of our men and boys died fighting not only for our own freedom but also in the shared struggle for independence of Colombia, Ecuador, Peru, and Bolivia—the building of republics of free and equal citizens.

Our people bled for the freedom of an entire continent. Freedom is in our essence.

This dialogue with the past—and with the duty we carry toward our country—was woven into my life from a very young age. We talked about it constantly around our kitchen table. The future I imagined for myself only existed in Venezuela—and only in a Venezuela that was free.

I am the oldest of four daughters, and I grew up determined to prove to my father that he did not need a son. My father was an extraordinary man—visionary, wise, generous, entrepreneurial, and a very successful businessman. From an early age, I decided I wanted to follow in his footsteps—to study what he studied and to become what he became. I set out to do just that, eventually taking on a role at the company my father led and working in Valencia, an industrial city just outside the capital where the company's main plants were located.

One day, in 1993, when I was pregnant—just days from giving birth—I returned to Caracas for a visit. When I arrived home, my mother told me she had been invited to a state institution for abandoned children. "It's ten minutes from our house," she said. "Why don't you come with me?"

I didn't even know the institution existed. But I went.

What I found was, in essence, a prison for children. The children were dirty and hungry. I felt overwhelmed with guilt.

How could something so horrific exist so close to my home without my knowing?

That day, I called my boss and told him, "I don't know if I'm coming back."

"What?" he said, surprised. "You love your job. You're on such a great trajectory here—one day you're going to do big things in this company."

I knew I would one day have to make a choice. Would I honor my father by following the path I had always imagined for myself—becoming a businesswoman and one day taking my father's place in the company? Or would I fight for freedom, democracy, and equality? I did not believe I could do both.

I told him I needed to do something first.

And I quit.

My mother and I began looking for volunteers. We created a foundation, and the work was incredibly difficult because the institution was controlled by the government. But we managed to sign what became a first-of-its-kind agreement—one that allowed civil society, through a private foundation, to take over the management of a state institution for at-risk youth who had been treated only as wards of the state.

Within that space, we reestablished a branch of the National System of Youth Orchestras. One of the children from that home would later play the violin with the Berlin Philharmonic.

That experience changed the course of my life—but it was only the beginning.

*

When Chávez was elected president in 1999, it was amid widespread public anger over corruption, inequality, and political disillusionment. A former military officer, presenting himself as an antielite socialist and having led a coup d'etat against a previous president, he promised to reestablish the republic, punish entrenched interests, and give power back to "the people."

By 2002 Chávez was already threatening fundamental freedoms—speech, association, and private property. Though he had been in power only a short time, his hostility toward the rule of law was unmistakable. He refashioned the constitution as soon as he got into power and used that popular mandate to dismantle democratic institutions from within, concentrating power in the presidency and laying the groundwork for an authoritarian system that would later deepen under Maduro.

I understood even then what he meant for Venezuela. And what I had to do.

A group of five friends and I—mostly engineers, as I was—began asking ourselves an essential question. If we were going to confront the regime peacefully, if we were determined to defend freedom and democracy without falling into violence, how could we give people a real way to decide the future of our country?

Our fear was real and justified. If we failed to find such a path, Venezuela was headed toward deeper authoritarianism—and inevitably, more violence.

The answer, we discovered, was already written into our constitution. It allowed citizens to subject any elected official, including the president, to a recall referendum once half of their term had been completed. To trigger such a vote, all that was required was the support of at least 20 percent of registered voters, expressed through their signatures.

And in our naïveté, we believed it would be simple. We imagined we would gather six signatures, then sixty—and that within two weeks we would have three million.

We collected six.

That was the moment we understood that if we wanted this to work, we had to think bigger, organize better, and operate at scale.

We created an NGO called Súmate—meaning "join us"—and began reaching out to people from every walk of life, across the country. Our message was *This is the hour of citizenship.* We need you. We need your voice. We need your work. Together, we can make the will of the people heard—but only if we organize and stand together.

But commitment alone would not be enough. If we wanted to transform people's energy into real power, we needed structure—organization, coordination, and grassroots mobilization.

So we set up call centers and asked Venezuelans to volunteer. Within a single month, thirty thousand people had contacted us. PhDs, mathematicians, teachers, technicians, all offering their skills and asking how they could help.

There was one call I will never forget. I was visiting the call center and picked up the phone. A woman was on the line. She said, "I work as a cleaning lady. The only thing I know how to do is clean. I offer myself to clean anything you need cleaned."

Her words, her humility, and her offer moved me profoundly. I took it as proof that we were on the right path—that the people were with us—and that, despite what everyone said, perhaps it was not impossible to gather the 2.4 million signatures we still needed.

This time, we set a single day to collect signatures. When that day arrived, we were terrified. Would anyone show up? Had we done enough? How many signatures would we get?

I still remember that morning like it was yesterday. Someone from my team called me. "María Corina," he said, "people are coming down the hills." They were coming down to join us. Caracas is encircled by hills, and it is in those hills that the poorest communities live, under the humblest conditions.

In a single day, we gathered more than enough signatures—over six hundred thousand beyond the threshold—and submitted them, forcing the regime, reluctantly, to acknowledge the petition.

But it refused to recognize the result. So we called on the country to sign again. And once again, millions of Venezuelans came out.

In the end, we succeeded in forcing a recall referendum, a direct constitutional challenge to Chávez's hold on power. What followed was a monumental fraud, carried out to prevent the will of the people from being expressed at the ballot box.

Still, it marked a turning point. Chávez understood that he had lost the country's support. He would respond by becoming even more violent, more authoritarian. And in that moment, I understood something, as well. Until then, I had been acting as a citizen, working through an NGO. I had done everything I knew how to do in civil society. But the situation demanded more. I could no longer stand on the sidelines, criticizing politics and politicians without being willing to step forward myself.

But the last thing I ever imagined doing was entering politics. I distrusted politics and politicians deeply. For years, I had been openly critical of the parties and the way politics was practiced in Venezuela. But by 2008 I felt we had reached the limits of what could be achieved from civil society alone. If I truly wanted to serve my country—and do things differently—I knew I would have to take the next step.

Around that time, I felt the need for distance and reflection. I accepted a fellowship at Yale, which gave me the space to look back on the path my life had taken—from the private sector, to social work, to the building of Súmate—and to confront a decision I knew would mark my life forever. I understood that there was no turning back, that choosing politics meant closing the door on the future I had always imagined for myself in the private sector, working alongside my father.

It was not an easy choice. I did not want to weaken Súmate, and I took that step alone. I even asked my staff to stay behind, not to follow me into whatever came next. By the end of my time at Yale, in December 2009, I knew the moment had arrived. When I returned to Venezuela in January 2010, I moved forward. Friends from my earliest years—women I had known since school—stood beside me as my campaign team, and together we took the first steps toward what would become a new political movement. At the time, I did not yet grasp what lay ahead: the construction of an entirely new political party.

Still, I worried deeply about betraying my father. It had long been my mission to follow in his footsteps. When I finally told him, he said, "Whatever you decide, I will support you. But I must warn you about what you are going to face. Are you truly aware of what lies ahead?" "Yes," I said, though I certainly wasn't.

Nonetheless, he supported me—steadfastly—even after all of his businesses were confiscated by the state. One day, some years later, he was sitting with my children, and I overheard him speaking to them. "We built a great thing," he said, speaking of his generation. "And you will have to do it all over again. But it will be even greater, because the generation of your mother is risking their lives for your freedom." Hearing those words gave me a deep sense of peace and the certainty that this fight was worth everything.

*

When I decided to run for the National Assembly, we started from nothing.

No party. No money. No political machinery. No institutional backing.

I had no formal political experience, which many people treated as a fatal flaw. Plus, I was a divorced woman and openly committed to ideas of individual freedom and open markets in a country conditioned by decades of state control. On paper, everything was against us. It was "impossible."

And yet, we won—not only the primary in my circuit, but the general election. In fact, we received the highest percentage of votes ever obtained by any candidate to the National Assembly. For me, this was another lesson in trusting the people—and further proof that Venezuelans were hungry for a different way of doing politics.

I entered Parliament with that sense of responsibility,

determined to call things by their name. I did not practice the traditional politics of calculation and silence. I spoke plainly. In fact, I was the first politician to call the regime what it was: a dictatorship. That carried a cost. The regime quickly made me a target—of attacks not only from the government, but also, at times, from within parts of the opposition, for whom proximity to me became politically risky.

That defiance infuriated the regime.

The turning point came in 2013, after a presidential election we believed had been stolen by Maduro. We denounced the fraud from the floor of the Assembly. During the session, the regime shut the doors of the building, cut the live broadcast, and ordered silence.

We were all trapped inside when the violence erupted.

I was standing in the chamber when I heard my name. I turned—and a proregime woman deputy struck me in the face, throwing me to the ground. The blow nearly rendered me unconscious. When I stood up and demanded that the Assembly be reopened, several deputies came at me from behind, pulled me by the hair, threw me down again, and kicked me repeatedly. My nose was fractured in four places.

The experience was incredibly painful, but brutal in its clarity: I was violently attacked inside the National Assembly of my own country.

That was the day I fully understood the true nature of the regime—and the impossibility of reforming institutions that had already been hollowed out. I saw, without illusion, that Venezuela did not suffer from a flawed political system but from a system designed to crush dissent and preserve power *at any cost.*

My time in Parliament confirmed a deeper conviction: Venezuela did not need another electoral tactic, but a new political culture—one rooted in citizens and ideas, not patronage and fear. A movement that believed the individual is not subordinate to the state but protected by it. So we founded Vente, my political party.

We were told such ideas would never resonate, especially among the poor. That they were abstract and elitist—impossible.

The people who told us that were wrong.

What we built—without money, without media, under censorship and attack—grew precisely because it spoke to values Venezuelans already held: human dignity, responsibility, freedom, cooperation, and trust. We invested not in slogans but in formation, debate, and ideas.

What once seemed impossible became real. And it was forged, above all, through courage.

Still, by 2022, there was a pervasive feeling of hopelessness, an exhaustion borne of years of repression and the regime's ruthless determination to cling to power.

From a civic perspective, we had tried everything. It seemed clear the regime intended to remain in power forever.

And yet, I had begun to sense something shifting. One day that year, as I was driving to the coastal state of Vargas, just outside Caracas, I asked a man for directions. He looked at me for a moment and said, "María Corina?"

"Yes," I answered.

"Could you step out of the car?"

I did. Suddenly, he took hold of my arms and began to cry.

"You are the only tool I have left to bring my children back home," he said.

I looked at him, and I began to cry too.

"And you," I told him, "are the only tool I have left to bring my children home as well."

In that moment, I said to myself, *This is it.* This is the force that will bring our country back together. This was not about a candidacy. It was not about an election. Anyone who thinks we are engaged in a purely political fight does not understand.

This is an existential struggle.

A spiritual struggle.

*

In the last few years, I have traveled hundreds of hours and thousands of kilometers around my country.

By 2023 I had been forbidden from leaving Venezuela for more than ten years, and for the previous six, I was not even allowed to board a domestic flight. What at first felt like a dreadful constraint became, in many ways, the greatest favor the regime ever did for me. It forced me to travel the country by car, by motorcycle, and on foot.

In trying to isolate me, they denied me the advantage of seeing Venezuela from above. But they left me with something far more valuable: the privilege of living it from within. I now know every road, every highway, every shortcut, every curve. I have eaten at *arepa* stands from one end of the country to the other. I have met with, marched alongside, listened to, and spoken with millions of Venezuelans. Together, we have endured so many struggles. We have lived through more than thirty elections—each one more fraudulent than the last.

Time and again, together, we have filled the streets with

millions of people. We have been shot at. Our young people have been killed or imprisoned. We have endured fifteen different "dialogue" processes with the regime—internationally mediated negotiations, usually convened after major protests and repression. And every time, Chávez and then Maduro followed the same script: they sent their international allies to negotiate. They would offer a great deal and gain time, money, resources, and the legitimacy that comes with appearing reasonable. And then they would violate every single promise made.

By that point, even the opposition parties were deeply discredited, and people felt profoundly disconnected from them. The pressure for real change had grown so intense that the parties had no choice but to accept something unprecedented: the citizens themselves would choose the new leadership.

Everything that had been tried before had failed. Elections, negotiations, dialogue processes—they had all become instruments of control, not change. What the primaries offered instead was something radically different: a way for people to reclaim ownership over their destiny.

Many forces did not want the primaries to happen, starting with the regime itself but also including entrenched interests within the opposition. Until the very last day, there were attempts to block them.

The campaign for the opposition primary was set to begin in six months, and everyone around us was saying the same thing: it was impossible—impossible—to unite the country around a legitimate leadership and a single aspiration for change. Impossible to reenergize a society that had been pushed into hopelessness. Impossible to rebuild trust among citizens.

But I had seen something different. I had seen, firsthand, what millions of Venezuelans were feeling. And I trusted the people.

That is why I agreed not only to support and promote the primary, but to run in it—under three non-negotiable conditions: there would be no involvement of the regime's electoral authority; the vote would be manual; and Venezuelans in the diaspora would have the right to participate. The primary winner would become the legitimate leader of the democratic opposition coalition and would face Maduro in a presidential election, should one take place.

It would not be an easy process. As is often the case under totalitarian regimes, portions of the traditional political opposition had been compromised or co-opted. Which is why, if any vote was going to be credible, it was so important to force power back into the hands of citizens. It had to be conducted in defiance of the system—a direct challenge to it. The regime thought there was no way we could organize something so complex and assumed fear would be enough to dissuade turnout because anyone who voted would be identified, marked, and punished. We had to prove them wrong.

It was an enormous effort—one whose full impact we did not yet fully understand. It would become the inflection point that set us on the path toward Venezuela's liberation. It was not something I could ever have done alone, and it is something I will never forget.

On October 22, 2023, around noon on Primary Election Day, I began receiving calls from all over the country. We had run out of paper ballots. Now, for the first time, I was the one saying it: *That's impossible.* We had printed three times as many ballots as we ever imagined we would need.

And yet people kept turning out. Thousands stood in line—in the rain, in the sun, under threats and fear. Many were furious because they could not vote.

I won with 92.3 percent of the vote.

Imagine what that meant to me—the responsibility. The mandate.

I had traveled the entire country telling people, *This is about you. This is about your responsibility. This is about what you need to do.*

I never promised anything for free. What I offered was hard work, sacrifice, and our commitment to bringing our children back home to a different nation. But everyone would have to do their part.

Responsibility and trust—that's what I had spoken about. Everywhere I went, I would say, "I trust you." And I would show it. I traveled without security. I walked among thousands of people. That was my testimony: I trusted them with my life, and I would earn their trust in return.

*

As soon as I won, the regime moved to bar me from the presidential ballot—despite a signed, internationally backed agreement in which they had accepted the rules and pledged to respect the primary's results. They did not. They knew exactly what we had built.

Instead, they announced that I would not be allowed to participate in the general election. Within hours, my core team was imprisoned—my chief of staff and those responsible for communications, elections, international relations, and political organization. In less than twelve hours, they dismantled what we had built over twelve years. It felt so unjust, so impossibly cruel to the millions of people who had fought so hard and risked so much.

I decided we would keep going. I prayed: "God, please. I need a name." And the name came to me: Corina Yoris—an eighty-year-old philosophy professor and a member of the primary commission. Her respect among civil society and academic credentials made her unobjectionable.

I asked her to take my place, and she agreed.

The regime blocked her too. They found technical excuses, but the message was clear: no one associated with that mandate would be permitted to run. Perhaps they feared even her name. Corina is not common in Venezuela. María Corina. Corina Yoris. They understood what people would see, and they wanted to take no chances.

So we kept searching for someone who could keep the movement intact and whom the regime might not immediately perceive as a threat.

That is how we arrived at Edmundo González, whose quiet integrity and distance from traditional politics became an unexpected source of strength.

González was a retired diplomat, seventy-five years old, a calm, honest, courageous family man. He had never been involved in partisan politics, and he was largely unknown to the broader public.

He was ideal, I thought. But first I had to convince him—and his family—to go along, because stepping forward carried real risk. Their lives would change forever. Edmundo understood the opportunity we had before us, the real possibility of victory. He agreed to run—and the regime, underestimating us once again, agreed to let him.

They believed that by allowing a candidate with no political trajectory to run—approved for the ballot barely three months before the election—it would be impossible for us to defeat them. I was determined to prove them wrong.

From that moment on, I traveled across the country carrying a poster with Edmundo's face, telling people: *If you want to vote for me, vote for him.* We worked together, sometimes for twenty hours a day, seven days a week. We went to the most remote corners of the country—places no politician had visited in decades, not because they offered the most votes, but because people there had been forgotten and needed to be seen and heard.

I traveled by car, as I always had—often driving myself. When the regime blocked the roads, people would appear with motorcycles, offering to take me to another point, where someone else was already waiting. In a single day, I might ride eight different motorcycles just to reach one town.

A journey that should have taken three or four hours could take seven, because every few hundred meters I had to stop to meet people—crying, pressing their babies into my arms, thanking me, protecting me, reminding me why we were there.

What emerged from those encounters was something deeply profound—spiritual, even intimate. Despite the thousands, and sometimes tens of thousands, who spontaneously gathered at our rallies, they never felt like crowds. They felt like one-on-one exchanges.

This was not a campaign of money or media. We had none. There were no ads, no television appearances, no interviews.

Everything was done through word of mouth, WhatsApp messages, and handwritten posters. Our rallies had no stages. I spoke standing on cars. People brought cardboard signs written with markers. Nothing was paid. Everything was given.

The final campaign rally before the election brought together almost two hundred thousand people in the streets of San Cristóbal. It was the largest public gathering in that city's history.

*

Since Chávez came to power in 1999, Venezuela has held more than thirty elections. Every one of those elections was manipulated—sometimes subtly, sometimes blatantly.

For years, we knew this, but we could never prove it.

This time had to be different.

We knew that winning by votes alone would never be enough. The margin had to be overwhelming—and the evidence undeniable. Even before the elections were officially announced that year, polling showed that a vast majority of Venezuelans were ready to vote to end Maduro's rule. The spirit of rejection was massive. But we also knew the regime would never accept defeat unless the truth was placed beyond its reach.

So we prepared for something unprecedented: to win—and to prove it.

Chávez used to boast that he had built the most sophisticated electoral system in the world. We had to outsmart it. In every polling center, votes are cast electronically, and when polling stations close, every machine prints an official tally sheet—a long strip of paper called an *acta*—signed by regime officials and by government and opposition witnesses—*testigos*—alike.

That *acta* is the truth. And by law, every witness has the right to an official copy.

Our entire effort came down to one instruction, repeated thousands of times across the country to our volunteers: get the *acta*, and guard it with your life.

For months before election day, entire communities mobilized into self-reliant civic networks, training one another in kitchens, churches, and living rooms. Instruction manuals were passed around like contraband. Even after every formal role had been filled, people still found ways to support the effort.

Traditionally, a nationwide voter-integrity effort in Venezuela requires at least ninety thousand trained citizens to serve as witnesses inside voting centers. Our goal was to recruit six hundred thousand volunteers to defend the vote. We got far more than that. Everyone claimed a piece of the effort, and in the end, more than one million people participated—directly or indirectly—in our operation.

And that was just the beginning.

On July 28, 2024—election day—millions of Venezuelans turned out to vote against the regime. They voted despite the threat of hunger—outside every voting center stood regime enforcers, reminding people that food subsidies depended on obedience. They voted knowing the violence the regime was capable of. They voted, in a word, for freedom.

Their votes were extraordinary acts of courage.

By six in the evening on July 28, as polling stations closed, results began to pour in from across the country—from urban centers and remote villages alike. Everywhere, the same numbers appeared: seventy to thirty.

We were stunned.

Then, suddenly, the flow of results slowed. We knew what that meant. Orders had gone out to expel our witnesses and block access to the *actas*.

More incredible acts of courage followed. Some people hid *actas* in their clothes. Others stayed locked in bathrooms until dawn. Soldiers disobeyed orders and looked the other way. Thousands risked detention, disappearance, or prison simply to carry a piece of paper out of a building.

Across the country, we had set up hidden processing centers, equipped with generators to survive blackouts, scanners to digitize the *actas*, and hidden satellite antennae to send them beyond the regime's reach. Volunteers worked in shifts through election night and into the next days, scanning, cataloging, and uploading each tally sheet before it could be confiscated or destroyed. In places without roads or connectivity, *actas* traveled by foot, canoe, or motorcycle—always one step ahead of the regime's grasp.

What the regime tried to control by force, Venezuelans answered with ingenuity.

By the next day, we had scanned and published 85 percent of all *actas*—enough to make the outcome mathematically irreversible. The data showed that Edmundo González Urrutia had won more than seven million votes, more than double Nicolás Maduro. Even if Maduro had somehow won every single vote we had yet to process, he would still trail Edmundo by more than a million votes.

The truth was visible to the world.

And yes, that very night, the regime announced fictional results—numbers written, as we say in Venezuela, "on a napkin." They claimed victory without evidence. To this day, they have never published the detailed results. We have. Any Venezuelan can see the tally from their own voting station, and anyone around the world can check the entire results database we published.

That is the proof.

And for that proof, people were hunted. Anyone known to have handled an *acta* became a target. Thousands of Venezuelans were disappeared, detained, and tortured in the aftermath of the elections. Some are still in prison today, simply for fulfilling their civic duty.

The victory of July 28, 2024, belongs to the millions of anonymous Venezuelans who trusted in each other in deciding to reclaim their future and the truth.

Freedom and the Future

We are living through the end of an old era and the beginning of a new one. I am profoundly grateful to God for having been born in this country and in this generation. We are writing history right now—and it is a bright page.

It has been a long journey—a long march toward freedom—since Venezuela was born as a nation, and we have not yet finished marching.

We are now fighting for the rebirth of our country. This is the task of our generation. Many Venezuelans of this time were born under a dictatorship, having known nothing else, and still they have chosen to risk their lives and their freedom for a democratic Venezuela. No generation has been better forged for the conquest of freedom than this one, and what we are doing now will echo for centuries to come.

We must also reconcile with every chapter of our history,

because each one has shaped who we are. We must take pride in them—even in our mistakes—because they forged a nation of many cultures and races, a country that has endured a very dark period and emerged united around shared values, the same values our founding fathers held from the beginning: dignity, justice, responsibility, equality before the law, family, and above all, freedom.

I am one among millions who have stood up and fought through these years. Thousands have been killed, tortured, exiled, or imprisoned. What we have done and sacrificed goes far beyond politics. It speaks to the virtues we want our children to embody and to the principles that unite us as a nation. Today, I believe there is no society in the world more cohesive than the Venezuelan people.

Ultimately, everything comes back to the people. We were able to do what we did because we trusted one another.

When I wrote the *Freedom Manifesto*, my purpose was to express the true nature of Venezuelan society: our civic courage, our dignity, and our capacity for love. Everything we have achieved was born from love—love for our country, love for freedom, and love for our children.

That is perhaps what it comes down to the most: the love for our children. Our responsibility toward them.

I used to be what we call in Venezuela a *mamá gallina*—a fiercely protective mother, always gathering her children close. After my divorce, my three children slept in my bed until they were quite old. And I often feel guilty for what I have brought upon my family. It is perhaps the most difficult burden I carry. I almost never speak about it; it is something I have not resolved in my own soul.

I remember a day early in my time in Parliament, fourteen years ago, when I began denouncing the mafia and the drug networks—something very few dared to do. Suddenly, my legs began to tremble, and my mouth froze. All I could think was, *My daughter is driving from her college to our home—alone* I sat down, unable to continue. When I got home, I told her, "You have to leave." She said, "I'm not leaving you." And I said, "Yes, you are. You must. I cannot do this while you're here."

The last night I slept in my own bed was the night before the July 28, 2024, election. I had every intention of returning home; I didn't even pack a bag. But I was forced into hiding. For sixteen months afterward, until only recently, I lived in strict self-confinement, interacting with the outside world almost entirely through a screen. While I was in hiding, a friend asked one of my sons about me, and he replied, "We have learned to live with this. But you must understand—if I call my mother and she doesn't answer or doesn't call back within five minutes, I am terrified."

And yet they have chosen to stand firm, despite the risks. I am profoundly grateful and proud of them. What I have seen in them—their strength, their clarity, their love—is impossible to describe. These extreme circumstances brought us together in a way I never imagined possible, especially across distance. I can tell you, truthfully, that I have never felt as close to my children as I have in those sixteen months.

My husband has also endured great hardship. He was forced to leave behind his law firm, his home, his career, and the life he had built, and to start again abroad. Throughout this ordeal, he has been my principal source of safety, comfort, and counsel—steady, patient, and unwavering when I needed it most.

In the end, the regime tried to tear us apart—and instead, it brought us closer together. It also changed us. I am a different person than I was just a few years ago. I am no longer impulsive. I have found a serenity I never imagined possible. I take one day at a time. Through this process, I have gained an inner peace. It comes from knowing we are doing the right thing.

One of the hardest things I have to do is call a mother in the middle of the night to tell her that her child has been detained and that we don't know where he or she is. At the same time, I receive letters from innocent young men and women in prison telling me they are strong and the fight is worth it. They ask me not to stop. They tell me to keep going. They say they are proud to be part of this movement. Imagine what I feel when I read those messages, coming from prison. Imagine what I feel when nuns write to tell me they woke up at three in the morning to pray for me.

"We're sending you our energy," they say.

So as hard as it has been, I don't want to be anywhere else.

*

When I won the Nobel Peace Prize, no one on Earth was more surprised than I was. I still can't quite believe it. I am proud of the people of Venezuela, who have worked and lost so much to deserve it.

It is a recognition of the struggle for democracy—and of democracy itself as an essential pillar of peace, something that must be remembered and defended every day.

Peace requires freedom. Freedom requires strength—not only moral strength but also spiritual strength, physical strength, and collective strength, exercised with discipline and responsibility, so that freedom can prevail.

That, to me, is what this prize represents. And that is why I believe it goes far beyond Venezuela.

It is a dedication to every citizen, anywhere in the world, who believes in freedom and dignity.

I am a practitioner of freedom—nothing more. And experience has taught me that freedom is fragile and that it is never free.

I believe every individual is born with the right to be free. It comes from our creation. It is not granted by circumstances, a political system, or another person. I have learned that even those who have never known freedom are willing to give their lives for it. That is what our young Venezuelans have taught us—the generation of our children. Many of them were born under this authoritarian regime, and yet they have been killed, imprisoned, persecuted, or exiled because they are determined to be free.

Freedom, above all, is an individual decision. To live in a free society, people must truly value freedom and understand what it demands—including the willingness to take risks with one's own life.

To be free, to exercise freedom, and to fight for it is a rational choice. But it requires constant vigilance, moral clarity, and as much hope as humanly possible.

People often tell me, "If you ever get rid of Maduro, it will take decades to build something new." To them I say, "Just wait and see. Very soon, you will witness what a free Venezuela is capable of achieving."

When Christopher Columbus arrived on the South

American mainland during his third voyage in 1498, he came ashore on Venezuela's Paria Peninsula. Overwhelmed by the exuberance and beauty of what he saw, he called it *Tierra de Gracia*—the Land of Grace.

That name captures the vision of the new Venezuela that is already emerging—not only because of its extraordinary natural richness but also, above all, because of the richness of its people: hard-working, respectful, joyful, faithful, and profoundly loving.

Venezuela will not only transform from a criminal hub of the Americas into the energy hub of the Americas—thanks to our immense endowments in oil, gas, and renewable resources—but also into a technological hub. We will use that energy to generate employment, innovation, and new opportunities for investment and prosperity for all.

But more importantly, Venezuela will become a beacon of hope—shining from within—because we will feel proud of what we accomplish together, as a nation, as families, and as a contribution to the world beyond our borders.

Few societies have fought as fiercely for their freedom as the Venezuelan people—for our own freedom and in solidarity with all nations that seek it. We have learned, through lived experience, what it means to receive support from others who share your cause. That lesson will remain with us forever.

When we win our freedom—and we will soon—every society on the planet should know that they, too, can be free.

Never give up.

Nothing is impossible.

FREEDOM MANIFESTO

Preamble

It became the sacred duty of the courageous Venezuelans to rise when our voices were silenced, our dignity denied, and our liberty shackled by the chains of tyranny.

We, the citizens of Venezuela, are not appealing to power or privilege, but rather to the eternal rights bestowed upon every human. It is from this foundation that truth is born: no ruler, faction or tyrannical force has the ability to dictate to individuals what is theirs by right: freedom.

Dignity is the catalyst that will elevate the Venezuelan's hearts and minds again. It will motivate hope and create a new world where our people will rise from this dark age of oppression with a single, unbreakable mission: freedom.

Because in a free republic the only sovereign is the people, because our popular and national sovereignty is inalienable, and because we Venezuelans know that freedom must be defended every day—there is no room for fear.

Therefore, let us relaunch a free society in which our

government serves and the state's primary purpose is to safeguard the natural rights of all Venezuelans.

The time has come for every Venezuelan family to be united again, forever, in our land.

Tomorrow Belongs to the Bold

We stand at the edge of a new era—one where our natural rights will prevail. This regime's long and violent abuse of power is ending.

A new Venezuela is emerging from the ashes, renewed in spirit and united in purpose, like a phoenix reborn—fierce, radiant, and unstoppable.

We will fully realize our potential, for the Land of Grace will safeguard our inalienable rights from future oppressive tyrannies, dictatorships, and despots.

Our individual liberty will forever be fully realized within a Venezuelan ecosystem booming with liberty.

Dignity: Our Guiding Principle

We hold that the dignity of every human soul is sacred—the first principle from which all liberty flows. The will to labor, to create, and to advance the common good is stimulated by dignity. An individual's self-worth grows through productivity; it elevates the human spirit, which, in turn, fortifies the entire community.

Let dignity serve as the driving force behind our national revitalization—the force that establishes a free marketplace of ideas and enterprise, that fosters the complete development of each individual, and that restricts the government's authority to its proper function as the steadfast guardian of our inalienable rights.

Every Venezuelan Is Born with Liberty

Freedom is not a privilege bestowed by a government; rather, it is an inherent right woven into the very essence of our humanity.

Every Venezuelan is born with inalienable rights that have been conferred upon them by our Creator, not by men. No regime, political system, or tyranny has the power to rob us of what is divinely ours: the right to live with dignity, speak freely, create, dream, and prosper as individuals.

Regenerate the Economy of a Free People

A renewed Venezuela will guarantee the right to own property and to reclaim what was stolen. Property is not a privilege of the elite; it is a fundamental right, the physical manifestation of a person's lifetime of labor and ingenuity.

Instead of unduly interfering, the government will provide the conditions to create a free and competitive economy.

Venezuela's prosperity depends on its citizens' freedom. History has proven that when government exerts a heavy hand on the marketplace, it suppresses the human spirit that provides genuine vitality for growth.

It is time to return power to the people, to the citizens, to the private sector.

We will awaken the economy that is capable of tripling its strength within a decade by releasing state-owned enterprises and restoring the development of our oil and gas sectors to the ingenuity of free men and women.

The wealth of Venezuela will never again be concentrated in the hands of a single, centralized power.

Envision a new Venezuela perched on top of the Western

Hemisphere, as the premier global energy hub—a symbol of independence and innovation. A new era of ingenuity in an open marketplace of ideas will catapult the next generation of leaders across all business sectors, including high-tech agribusiness, eco-friendly tourism, fintech, artificial intelligence, robotics, rare earth minerals, and defense.

A nation where each citizen can engage in commerce without government restriction, think independently, and receive fair compensation from their inventions and the fruits of their labor—such is the promise of a self-reliant people, people free to build, to prosper, and to lead.

For let us remember, history has proven, when individuals are prosperous from their labor, all other human rights follow.

Freedom of Speech

The right to speak the truth is the cornerstone of all freedom. When voices are suppressed, corruption takes hold, and justice disappears.

Venezuela must reclaim its voice in every town, classroom, newsroom, and digital environment. The people must be able to speak without fear of persecution, censorship, or reprisal.

Venezuela's advancement in this next era depends entirely on the unrestricted exchange of ideas and the courage to speak them.

Right to Vote

The ballot box serves as the people's defense against oppression. It is sacred.

Every Venezuelan must have the right to vote securely and without any form of manipulation.

Our vote is our collective voice. The will of the people must be reflected in elections, rather than the power of the few.

Let Venezuela's elections reflect the full expression of our popular sovereignty and never as tools of subjugation.

Right to Assemble

The streets belong to the people—not to the illegitimate power. The heartbeat of democracy is the right to assemble, protest, and stand together in unity. The peaceful assembly of citizens does not pose a threat to a nation; rather, it fortifies it.

Venezuela's rebirth will commence when each of us can emerge from hiding, walk from the shadows without dread, and wave flags of hope.

The Right to Safety

Every individual has the right to safeguard their life, their family, their property, and their liberty. No democratic society can endure when its citizens are incapable of resisting oppression or violence.

The people of Venezuela deserve a duly elected government that maintains the will and capacity to guarantee the safety of every citizen.

The future of Venezuela requires the restoration of trust between the state and its citizens. This will be achieved by promoting a lawful self-defense and fostering a culture of mutual respect, responsibility, and peace.

Therefore, we will reform our military and police forces so that their mission, sacred purpose, and constitutional duty is to defend all people of Venezuela as well as our national territory.

Bring Them Home Now

Nine million Venezuelans have been forced to flee their homeland, leaving behind families and friends—dreams shattered.

We will bring them home. We will restore their right and liberty to return—to come back to their native land.

Each Venezuelan must regain their family, their home, and their own future.

Crimes Against Humanity

The cries of the murdered, tortured, and disappeared have echoed unanswered for too long.

Since Maduro assumed power, more than eighteen thousand political prisoners have suffered—each one serves as a testament to the regime's brutality.

These are human lives: our friends, families, colleagues and companions.

The world must not turn its back. The criminal regime must be held accountable.

Venezuela will only fully rise when those who committed crimes against humanity are held accountable by both the law and history.

Education Must Rise Again

Venezuela's schools and universities must once again be the nucleus of curiosity, knowledge, and pride—the driving force behind progress. The classrooms of a nation are the source of its future.

Our children must be empowered to become a nation of leaders, innovators, and thinkers; Venezuela will do so by investing in our educators, technology, innovation, and the truth.

Our schools and universities of the future will leave today's culture of corruption forever in the past.

Families, as the first community, are the foundation of all education, instilling values, cultivating virtues, and shaping honorable citizens through their daily example.

Protect Venezuela's Land

The destruction of Venezuela's rainforests is not only an environmental catastrophe but also a moral one. The permanent destruction of our forests, rivers, and biodiversity deprives our children and grandchildren of their rightful inheritance.

A free Venezuela must also protect its land and extraordinary natural endowments.

Return to the International Community of Democracies

Venezuela will strengthen through international cooperation and collaboration.

We look forward to the day we return to the global stage with transparency, integrity, and purpose. We must reestablish alliances founded on shared prosperity, defense of democracy, environmental stewardship, trade, and human rights.

We will become a pillar of democratic and energy security in the Western Hemisphere, and the unwavering promoter of liberty around the world.

—María Corina Machado
Venezuela, November 9, 2025

VOICES OF VENEZUELA

A Note from María Corina Machado

The stories you are about to read are a portrait of a country.

They are the stories of mothers who seek justice for their children. Of environmental defenders protecting our ravaged land. Of workers, human rights advocates, community leaders, and campaign volunteers who chose to stand upright when it would have been easier—and safer—to remain silent.

These men and women did not step forward seeking recognition. Many had never participated in public life before this struggle demanded something of them. They acted because they understood that when a nation's dignity is attacked, neutrality is no longer possible.

In these pages, you will encounter pain, and you will surely feel outrage. You will also encounter something stronger than fear: determination. Conviction. Love. A determination rooted in love for family, for community, and for a country that refuses to surrender to repression and corruption.

In Venezuela today, courage has names. It has faces. It has families. And it has consequences.

The Venezuelan democratic movement has been built by ordinary citizens who refused to accept that authoritarianism was their destiny. These testimonials reflect that collective effort. They reveal the cost of defending the right to choose, the right to speak freely, and the right to live without fear.

No political transition is sustained by leaders alone. It is sustained by citizens willing to protect the truth, even at personal risk. The individuals who share their experiences here represent millions more whose stories remain untold: those still imprisoned, those in exile, and those who continue their work inside Venezuela under constant threat.

These pages carry those voices, voices that matter because of what they have endured and because of what they are determined to build: a Venezuela founded once again on dignity, justice, individual responsibility, and democratic coexistence.

These testimonials were recorded in December 2025, while I was still in hiding in Venezuela, when many families were living under the threat of persecution and imprisonment—a threat that still remains. In Venezuela, Christmas is a deeply cherished time of extended family, music, memory, and tradition. For too many, it has also become a season marked by absence: empty seats at the table, loved ones in exile or behind bars.

May these stories remind us that even in the darkest hours, there are citizens prepared to defend freedom with integrity and courage.

And may we never forget that it is with and for them that we will rebuild our republic.

Rosa Orozco

In early 2014 Venezuela experienced the largest wave of protests since Nicolás Maduro came to power. What began as student demonstrations against crime, shortages, and economic collapse quickly spread across the country. Hundreds of thousands of young Venezuelans took to the streets, demanding democratic freedoms and respect for their rights.

The government responded with force. The National Guard, intelligence services, and armed civilian groups were deployed to suppress the demonstrations. That year, more than forty people were killed during protests, hundreds were injured, and thousands were detained. The events of 2014 marked the beginning of a new phase of repression in Venezuela.

On February 19, 2014, in the city of Naguanagua in Carabobo state, a group of National Guardsmen on motorcycles opened fire near a residential area. Among those struck was twenty-three-year-old Geraldin Moreno, a university student and high-performance athlete.

This is her mother Rosa's testimony.

I am the mother of Geraldin Moreno, a young woman killed during the 2014 student-led protests.

From then on, we began this hard, torturous, difficult task of continuing the pursuit of justice.

I don't know whether to start by saying that I was an ordinary mother like all mothers.

I am an industrial relations technician. I worked—like all mothers in this country—to support my daughter, Geraldin.

That was a very beautiful twenty-three-year relationship I had with my daughter until she left.

I worked like any normal person in this country. We lived in Naguanagua, in a housing development in Tazajal. That was my life: working for my daughter so that she would have a good future—like any mother, like how I was raised, like how my own mother was raised, where you have to instill values, where you have to have a sense of responsibility for where you are, for what you live, and for what you have.

We are very religious; we believe in life and in God above all else. For us, I believe—no, I am convinced—that all of this is a project God had for all Venezuelans, where He taught us to believe more in ourselves and to work more for the country and to say, "This is the country we have, the only one we have, and we must keep fighting for it, for its sake."

*

Since day one, we have always protested. We never—I never—and my family never agreed with Hugo Chávez when he arrived, and we always went out to protest because we did not agree with what was happening. So we, all my nephews, Geraldin, and I—always went out to protest together. All the kids were little, so that's why many of our family's T-shirts say, "My mother taught me to fight," because I taught her to fight for this country, to believe in this country. It's the only one we have, and we must defend it.

My house was always full of kids. Geraldin was very chatty, very friendly. She joined every activity. I would tell her, "We have Father's Day," and she was already involved; She was too for Mother's Day, Christmas, any holiday—whatever it was. She loved animals. She loved sports. She was a high-performance soccer player, and she was a very joyful girl.

And she was the first granddaughter on both sides—on her father's side and mine. She was the one who would arrive and bring the party to the house.

She loved to dance, to go out with her friends.

She was the joy of the house. My apartment is fifty-seven square meters, and now it feels like a mansion because it's huge without her.

She was a child for whom I achieved everything I wanted.

*

Being a mother is not easy, because no mother carries an instruction manual under her arm telling her what's right or wrong. But depending on how you were raised, the values instilled in you—I raised her with good feelings. One of the things Geraldin hated most in the world was going to the supermarket. At that time, in 2013, food shortages meant there were long lines of people, especially elderly people, standing in line to try to get milk or eggs. And she would get very upset seeing an elderly person waiting. So she would sit an old man down to rest and stand in line for him. Or if they wouldn't sell a liter or two liters of milk to an elderly person, she'd tell me, "Buy a liter of milk." We didn't even drink milk. "Buy a liter."

She hated seeing the injustices happening, and that's why her entire generation went out to the streets to demand justice and freedom and respect for their rights. That's what protesters would say: "Respect my rights." But unfortunately, look what happened.

Geraldin was studying technology at Arturo Michelena University in 2014; she was graduating at the end of that year. Geraldin had her life very well planned. At the end of the year, she was going to Canada to pursue a postgraduate degree in cancer cell research, and she was going to study there because she wanted to open a clinic in Margarita, a Venezuelan island.

We were going to move to Margarita, but it didn't happen.

*

She always went out to protest with me, and we'd been protesting for several weeks together. But there came a moment when I couldn't keep up with the drive the students had. And that was a worry. "Where are you? What are you doing?" I had many friends I would tell, "I need you to go to search the avenues in Valencia—Cedeño, the shopping center, El Trigal, the overpass—find Geraldin, and bring her home." They were on motorcycles. "Pick up Geraldin, and bring her home." It would be midnight, one, two, three in the morning, and she still wasn't home.

The one day I told her not to go out was the day everything happened—the 19th of February—right at our doorstep, when they shot her at point-blank range. That day I told her not to go out, and she told me she wasn't going to because they were just returning from Génesis's funeral. Génesis was twenty-two years old and got shot in the head by paramilitaries the day before, during a protest. Génesis's younger sister was Geraldin's friend and lived behind us in another housing development in

Tazajal. They were coming from the funeral, and they decided to go out, and look what happened. That day, they hadn't even gone out to march. They were just standing right in front of the house like neighbors did every morning at 8:00 a.m., banging on pots and waving flags to protest from their homes since day two of when this wave of protests began. And that's when a group of thirteen motorcycles arrived, the riders shooting.

*

It changed everything.

First and foremost—and this is a major goal I have for the new Venezuela we will have—everyone must learn about human rights because we don't know anything about that. In 2014 I didn't know what human rights were, what my rights were, or what my daughter's rights were. My daughter knew because she was in university, and students knew why they were protesting. That's another thing: they protested with a basis, not because you go out to protest without reason—no. They wanted freedom, democracy, and respect for their rights.

And that's when the maternal instinct began—supporting other mothers, other wives, other sisters, gathering to denounce what was happening. Thirteen motorcycles arrived at my home. They came to my home carrying twenty-four or twenty-five National Guards, all firing their guns. And out of the twenty-five National Guards, only two officers have been sentenced—those who fired the weapons. And the others, who saw them shoot Geraldin, where are they? They are accomplices—whether or not they're considered "necessary" accomplices under the law. You saw what happened, and you stayed silent. Where is the chain of command? Someone gave the order, someone received the order, and someone executed it. Where are they? So that has been our work. It has been very hard.

Geraldin has been dead eleven years and ten months.

We have done everything possible and impossible, and we will continue doing so, denouncing nationally and internationally everything that has happened in Venezuela. More than four hundred young people have been killed in protests since 2014. Many mothers have not even been called to a hearing, not even told, "Here is the supposed culprit." Not even that.

So that has been my work since my daughter was murdered: telling families, "If you don't speak out, if you don't denounce, nothing will happen." That was my work. I denounced my daughter's case anywhere I could. Anywhere and everywhere I could, I submitted written statements stamped by the prosecutor's office. Every year on the anniversary of Geraldin's death, I go there with a document requesting the prosecution of the entire chain of command and all National Guardsmen who were there. They stamp it, and they sign it.

"You're not accomplishing anything with that," they tell me.

"Yes, I am. I take this everywhere I can."

I want justice in my country, and I will go wherever I must to present it. That is my work with victims. That's why in 2017, Justicia, Encuentro y Perdón (Justice, Coming Together, and Forgiveness) was founded. As its name says justice, because all families want justice; coming together, because Venezuela needs reconciliation among us; and forgiveness, which is a very strong and difficult word, but one we all need.

Forgiveness for ourselves, so that we can move forward,

because this is not easy, and from here on, everything will get even harder. But we can continue working because Venezuelans have incredible resilience. We can move forward, and we will achieve it—if we unite, like families have united, whether because of killings or political imprisonments, we can lift this country up.

It is very important that no Venezuelan families—none of them—carry hatred in their hearts. And if you don't have hatred in your heart, you can move forward, you can help rebuild this country.

When we were in the clinic, when Geraldin was in intensive care, I was with my mother and my aunts. You know mothers have a sixth sense; they know their children very well. My mother sat beside me and told me, "You have two paths. You can choose forgiveness and reconciliation, because that's what you taught your daughter, and choose love. Or you can choose hatred and retaliation against those people, and with that you won't achieve anything. I assure you that if you forgive yourself and move forward, you will achieve much more." And that was the advice I took from my mother.

*

In the courtroom, during one of the trials, I took the chance—since the prosecutors, my lawyer, and the military's lawyers weren't there, but the soldiers were—I approached them from behind and said to them: "Why did you shoot Geraldin? What was the reason? Why did you shoot her?"

One of them broke down crying, and the other looked at the floor.

I told them, "Fine, you don't want to say anything. Don't say it. But I am going to tell you something: I am going to forgive myself, because I need to forgive myself to move forward, and I will forgive you, too. Because you have children, and your children don't deserve to live what they are living now." And I don't want to carry the weight of children looking at me like people look at Jorge Rodríguez or Delcy Rodríguez—two of the government's top officials associated with repression, whose own father died in government custody—growing up their whole lives with hatred because of their father's death.

And I don't want that for myself, for Venezuela, or for any young person or child. Because one of the things I most value, love, and must keep fighting for is children—this Venezuelan youth who need us. Everything that happened is our fault for not having the vision and responsibility to leave the country in better hands. And that's what happened. And look at the consequences—look at everything that happened with all these young people who died.

So I forgave myself. And I swear that when I returned to my seat to wait for the trial to start, I took a deep breath. That was in 2015, and from then on, I have been able to move forward. It is one of the hardest things, and I continue working on it, because forgiving is not easy. But it is the work one must do to move forward.

Every morning, I give her a *bendición*; I pray for her to be blessed. It's very sad, but that's how it is.

Sometimes I don't want to get up, but it's like a little whisper in my ear saying, "Mom, get up. Mom, we have to keep going. Mom, you have to keep doing what you taught me: loving this country, loving people, and working so you can move forward."

I don't want to listen, I don't feel like it, but then I get a call from a student or a young person who tells me, "Mrs. Rosa, we need your help, there's something we need to get done," and I laugh and say, "Alright, you win. I'll get up."

They always find a way to show up.

What I loved most was taken from me—half of my life, half of my heart left with her.

But every morning when I go out and see the sun, feel the breeze on my face, see a child playing, or see a university student, a young person who is twenty or twenty-three years old, I see my daughter reflected in them. Because that could have been Geraldin, that could have been her path, and it is our duty to move forward for Venezuelan youth.

It is very important because that is the future of this country. That is the raw diamond we must continue polishing throughout life, as long as we have strength and health. That's why democracy, freedom, and rights must be our priority from now on, because we are going to recover the country. We are already recovering it, but we need people beside those who will rebuild this country—whatever small contribution we can make, whatever grain of sand we can give. "You have a job, you're working, great—but give at least one or two hours to the country," because the country needs it, and we all need it. We need to rebuild the country, and it won't be the Venezuela I knew—it will be a better Venezuela.

A country where we can sit and say, "We did it. Thank God, we did it," and we must keep going for that.

Geraldin Moreno was killed on February 19, 2014, during protests in Carabobo state. Two National Guard officers were later convicted for firing their weapons. No broader accountability has followed.

Marta Tineo

For more than a decade, Venezuela has endured widespread human rights violations documented by the United Nations, the Inter-American system, and independent organizations: extrajudicial killings, arbitrary detentions, enforced disappearances, torture, and systematic persecution of dissent. Domestic institutions have failed to ensure effective investigations or accountability, leaving victims with little recourse inside the country.

In that landscape of impunity, civil society has assumed roles normally carried by functioning justice systems—documenting abuses, preserving evidence, accompanying victims, and seeking justice beyond Venezuela's borders. Marta Tineo is one of the lawyers who chose to stay and carry that work forward.

This is Marta's story.

I am a lawyer, a graduate of the Central University of Venezuela. At that same university, I completed a specialization in human rights, then a postgraduate master's in criminalistics—the study of criminal investigation—and later in international justice systems.

In 2014 Rosa Orozco, the mother of Geraldine Moreno, a young woman killed during the 2014 protests in Venezuela, met with a group of families who had suffered similar losses. She reached out to me for legal support—I was then a human rights lawyer—and we began working together informally, without any structure. I assisted these victims legally and helped document their cases, and in February 2017 we formally established Justicia, Encuentro y Perdón.

Justicia, Encuentro y Perdón is a civil society organization dedicated to documenting and presenting cases of grave human rights violations before national and international bodies. But we do so not only to pursue justice. We also understand that Venezuela's longstanding human rights crisis, which has lasted more than a decade, is deeply tied to the breakdown of the social fabric, to polarization, to the government's aggressive policy against civil society, to intolerance and resentment—to that constant rhetoric of confrontation, of seeing an "internal enemy." That is the root of the crisis.

So we also work to rebuild the social fabric. That's why the word *encuentro*—"encounter"—is part of our name. And *perdón*—"forgiveness"—as well.

After founding the organization, I realized our work couldn't be limited to the legal field, even though that was my background. Direct contact with victims showed me that we needed a broader approach—a *psycho-legal* perspective.

That led me to train—with the support of Andrés Bello Catholic University and the Central University—in *psychological first aid*, in a program beautifully named Accompaniment in Pain and Crisis. This training came from the need to support victims not only by documenting and submitting their cases to international justice institutions but also by walking with them—humanly, empathetically—giving them the tools to stay grounded in their pain, to resignify it, and to transform it into strength in their pursuit of justice.

As part of this work, I trained with Colombia's *Fundación para la Reconciliación*, which has over thirty years of experience supporting victims of that country's armed conflict. They created a methodology called Schools of Forgiveness and Reconciliation. It is aimed at victims of violence—not only political or institutional but also social and personal. The method focuses on healing wounds caused by all types of violence—whether from the state or from society—and on guiding people through the process of forgiveness.

And I must emphasize that forgiveness does not mean renouncing justice. On the contrary, forgiveness means freeing oneself from hatred and resentment, while remaining conscious of the wound and remembering it. That is why memory is central to all our work.

Within the organization, we have a component devoted entirely to memory, because memory repairs the victim morally by honoring their story and it also gives society awareness of the magnitude of the harm done. In countries that seek *guarantees of nonrepetition*—a term in transitional justice frameworks—memory carries a double value: it repairs and it prevents.

I first trained in the Schools of Forgiveness and Reconciliation as a participant, and later I was selected by the foundation to train as an international facilitator. This allowed me to conduct forgiveness and reconciliation workshops in Venezuela with groups of victims we accompany, and also with others who have endured different forms of violence.

So that is both my professional and my human practice. As I said, I began accompanying victims, and the work expanded in many directions. Ultimately, our mission combines the pursuit of justice with the reconstruction of the social fabric, whereby victims play the leading role. These processes must aim to overcome pain—to resignify it and transform it into a force for good, not into hatred or vengeance. Hatred only fuels the endless cycle of violence, turning victims into new victimizers. That cycle must end.

Only through a culture of peace and national reconciliation—without ever abandoning justice—can we move forward. Justice remains our principal goal. It is not optional; it is a vital need.

Since my law studies, I always knew I would become a human rights defender. That is why I chose this path and immediately specialized in human rights. There is a deep personal calling in me to promote and defend them.

*

Being Venezuelan, having done all my professional training here, I have been stubbornly committed to staying in my country, even through times of institutional collapse, poverty, persecution, pain, and anguish. Still, I have done everything possible and hope to continue, to remain here. I feel this is where I belong—with a responsibility that is not only personal but also historical—standing beside victims.

For me, it is essential to be here, accompanying them and seeking justice. I believe in justice. And I believe that as Venezuelans, we have learned so much—how to grow through pain, how to resignify it, how to practice solidarity. We have learned from our mistakes, and that gives us strength to rebuild ourselves as a nation.

For me, standing with victims—empathizing with their pain, helping them find meaning and purpose—has been fundamental. It has changed how I see life and how I relate to others. I cannot imagine doing anything else, or being anywhere else, but beside those who have suffered the worst of Venezuela's human rights crisis. They are my teachers—examples of dignity, resilience, and strength. My role is to give back some of that strength and help them navigate these processes. It is a privilege to walk with them.

On a personal level, the pain sometimes breaks you. This work never stops. Every day, full time, we listen to stories of pain and horror. International human rights bodies have documented them thoroughly—killings, arbitrary detentions, enforced disappearances, torture, sexual violence, even sexual slavery. All the horrors that can be committed against humanity, we have sadly documented in Venezuela.

Of course, it takes an emotional toll—deep exhaustion at times. But just when you feel you can't continue, you receive a call from a mother, a sibling, a spouse, a child—and you think: *If they can keep standing, how could I give up?*

Yes, there is fear. Yes, there is anxiety. And yes, human rights defenders in Venezuela have been imprisoned simply for exercising the *right to defend human rights*, which is itself a human right. We work under that threat. But an even greater fear drives us: that everything remain in impunity, that victims be left without support, without hope for justice or reparation. That fear turns into strength.

This work changes your life. You learn to adapt: there are places you can't go because it's too risky; you change routines, even family ones. There are consequences, of course. But I believe it is worth it. I've had the support of my family. And again, the strength of the victims themselves keeps me going.

*

I think the greatest lesson is that above hatred, cruelty, and evil, there is a much stronger force: *love.*

Love is what sustains you. When I speak to mothers whose children were killed and I can't imagine a deeper pain, they tell me, "I want justice. I will fight to honor my child's name, to clear their story, so no other mother suffers what I have suffered." You realize that love can overcome anything.

The same is true with families of political prisoners. They live in constant anguish, yet they persist: "We must continue." They never abandon their loved ones.

The great lesson, I think, is this: human beings can destroy themselves through hatred or rebuild themselves through love. Love endures everything—not only love for family or friends but also for a country. From that love comes resilience, courage, and purpose. Because, in the end, this work is for our country, for our people—and that gives it meaning.

*

If we have learned anything, it is the cost of denying the other. The lesson must be that rebuilding a country is only possible through absolute respect for human dignity.

If there is one thing that has been repeatedly attacked for decades, it is dignity. And I believe we have learned that dignity is sacred. What calls us now is to recover it—not only individually, but collectively, as a nation. To recover our dignity and ensure that never again will anyone in our country be stripped of theirs.

For that, we must be conscious of the harm done, not to dwell in victimhood but to make sure it never happens again.

It's not only "forbidden to forget," as we often say—it's *never again.*

May all this pain become a permanent reminder that we must never again allow anyone—through power, ideology, or indifference—to take away our personal or national dignity.

María Franco

In December 2019, amid escalating conflict over illegal mining and military control in Venezuela's remote southeastern state of Bolívar, thirteen members of the Pemón Indigenous community were arrested after the alleged assault of a military outpost in the village of Luepa.

The Pemón people live in the Gran Sabana, a vast jungle and savanna region bordering Brazil and Guyana—a territory larger than many European countries, with communities separated by hours of unpaved roads and limited state presence except for the armed forces.

Before any investigation took place, Nicolás Maduro publicly accused the Indigenous detainees of rebellion and theft of military weapons. Human rights organizations documented enforced disappearances, torture, and severe procedural violations.

Salvador Franco, a community carpenter and father, was one of those detained. This is his daughter María's story.

My dad was a wonderful man, and he was a wonderful father.

He was a carpenter—he worked as a carpenter for the community.

That night—when everything started—I remember he was talking with my mom. And because I respected him, I didn't want to listen to anything he was talking about.

He went out that night—it was December 19th, I think. And he disappeared, for like two or three days.

I remember that about two or three days passed, and he came back just for a little while, and then he left again. I didn't ask where he was going or whom he was with—nothing like that.

And at dawn, we were asleep—all of us. It was like four or five in the morning, and we heard gunshots.

We all ran out of our houses. When my mom heard it, she told us to stay inside—not to go out. She went outside.

I went out too, to see what was happening. I went to the little store, right there by the road on Troncal 10, the road that leads to the Brazilian border. I peeked out, and there were lots of gunshots, National Guards—a crowd of people.

And then I went back home. We stayed there the whole day.

They told us they had taken my dad and that he was being held at Kilometer 80, a military-controlled zone. They locked him up. And then they said he had escaped through the mountains—through the bush. He walked until he reached another village farther ahead of ours. He stayed there—he was around there for about five days, wandering through the savanna, until he reached a point when he went to a friend of his—supposedly a friend. And that day, I think the friend went to the guards to tell them he was there.

So they went to get him, the SEBIN, the secret police.

They put him in a black bag. They beat him with weapons, kicked him. My mom told me they shocked him with electricity all over his body. He spent two days there. Then a helicopter came, and they took him to Caracas, to the place past San Rafael. I don't know what it's called.

He worked as security in our community. I think that's why they took him—they thought he was part of their group. They grabbed him and took him away.

We weren't allowed to leave our house. No information. We knew nothing about him—nothing.

And I remember they took him to Caracas. They locked him in a basement—he was there for about a month, I think. In that basement, he didn't eat—nothing, nothing. They mistreated him a lot.

That's all I remember.

*

I traveled to see him on the 20th of December of that year. But I couldn't see him. They didn't let me in.

I spoke with him the night before—to tell him I was going there. I told him everything—that I was in Caracas, that I was going to see him. And he told me, "OK, give me your ID number so they can register you when you come."

But I was fourteen. They didn't let me in because of that. Because I was a minor.

Two of my aunts, my dad's sisters, were with us. They told us he was sick—that he had tuberculosis. When we got to the prison, my aunt asked about his health. The guards told her he was fine—that everything was fine.

But he was vomiting a lot. My aunt wanted to get him taken to a hospital, but the guards said no—that he couldn't be moved.

After they didn't let me in, I talked to him on the day we came back home to our village. He told me many things—he told my mom to send him the Bible, things like that. That's all I knew.

A week later, my aunt told us she was going to Caracas to see him because of his health. When we heard about his illness, we felt awful. They told us it was because of the mistreatment he received.

And I remember he died on January 3rd. It was a very sad message. Really sad.

*

In the beginning, it was very hard for us. We lived with a void in our hearts for about a year—missing our dad, everything. It was really hard for us.

It's something very, very sad for me—talking about this case. I told my mom that I never wanted to talk about it again.

*

I want my dad's case to help—to help us get support, everything related to his case. It was something very hard for us.

Being with him was the most special thing. Just being with him.

And I want to tell everyone who has their father alive—appreciate him, hug him—because you never know when he'll be gone.

Salvador Franco died in state custody on January 3, 2020. No official investigation has resulted in accountability.

Cristina Burelli

Southern Venezuela forms part of the Amazon basin—one of the planet's largest carbon sinks and a critical regulator of South America's water and climate systems. The region contains vast protected national parks, ancient geological formations, and Indigenous territories long insulated from industrial activity.

Over the past decade, the Orinoco Mining Arc, a state-sanctioned zone spanning over 111,000 square kilometers, has brought widespread deforestation, mercury contamination, the resurgence of malaria in previously controlled zones, and the entrenchment of armed groups who control mining camps through coercion and forced labor.

In 2018, Cristina Burelli co-founded SOS Orinoco to document and map this transformation.

This is Cristina's story.

The situation in southern Venezuela is terrible—worse every day. Despite everything we've achieved with SOS Orinoco—documenting and presenting evidence of unprecedented environmental destruction—none of it has changed the criminal behavior of Nicolás Maduro's regime.

They continue promoting criminal mining. There are more mining accidents every day, more evidence of mining footprints—we can prove it with satellite images. Nothing has stopped. Satellite analysis shows that mining has affected thousands of hectares of protected rainforest, including more than two thousand hectares around Yapacana National Park alone.

We believe Maduro and his circle—Cilia Flores, Delcy Rodríguez—all of them are "scraping the pot." They know they're leaving, and they're extracting everything they can. They're looting the Amazon. It's the same behavior.

When I was thirteen years old, I went on a trip with my father and Charles Brewer-Carías, a Venezuelan explorer and naturalist, to Roraima—a flat-topped mountain in southeastern Venezuela, one of the oldest geological formations on Earth. I wasn't invited, obviously. But I had read Brewer's book about Roraima, so I told my father that I was going on that trip with him. It was an experience that marked me and set me on a path.

In 2018, when rumors began that Chinese groups were supposedly mining in Canaima—a UNESCO World Heritage site famous for Angel Falls—images started circulating on Instagram claiming the Chinese had mines at the base of the waterfall. I started calling people—journalists and academics—to understand what was going on. I quickly realized two things: first, there was a lot of fear; second, people had no way of proving what was being rumored. Only some journalists had bits of information.

So I contacted UNESCO, because Canaima is a World Heritage Site. But they knew nothing. They weren't informed. They were only getting the regime's narrative. Multiple independent analyses have confirmed mining activity inside Canaima and other protected areas, with maps showing at least fifteen illegal gold mining sites inside the park's boundaries.

Chavismo imposed a narrative about its Indigenous and environmental policies—a "revolutionary" story that presented the regime as an environmental champion defending native peoples and the Amazon. And it became accepted as truth.

So in 2018 when we started uncovering all this, it was very difficult to counter that narrative.

It was very hard internationally to bring this news forward—that the Orinoco Mining Arc was a massive scheme for looting the country's mineral wealth through illegal and state-sanctioned mining operations.

The Orinoco Mining Arc covers more than 12 percent of Venezuela's territory, over 111,000 square kilometers, and has been widely documented as a center of legally sanctioned and illegal mining activity that has encroached on multiple national parks and Indigenous lands.

With SOS Orinoco—which I founded in 2018 with a small group of Venezuelan experts—the idea was to report and document everything factually, using satellite imagery because it's very difficult—and prohibited—to access these areas.

The first report was anonymous, and what we found was terrible: over one thousand hectares of illegal mining inside Canaima National Park. And the same pattern repeated in other parks: Yapacana, Upper Orinoco, Caura, etc.

We sent the first report to UNESCO. The only way we could do this was anonymously. And they agreed. They said, "No problem—as long as the report is technical. We're used to working with authoritarian governments."

We uncovered something terrible. Over time I took the risk of becoming the public spokesperson for SOS Orinoco. I knew that by doing so, I would never be able to return to Venezuela. But I understood that to bring this situation to light, someone had to speak publicly on behalf of a team that kept growing—a network of people inside Venezuela risking their lives every day.

My risk is that I can't go back to Venezuela. But at least I can speak. They can't.

Gerardo Leal

In Venezuela, motorizados*—motorcycle couriers and self-employed transport workers—are embedded in their neighborhoods and often serve as informal networks of communication and mobilization. During years of economic collapse and fuel shortages—even in one of the world's largest oil-producing countries—many organized around access to gasoline and basic survival needs, drawing scrutiny from local authorities.*

By 2024, as María Corina Machado's campaign gained momentum, motorcyclists across the country began accompanying her rallies in spontaneous caravans that supporters referred to as a "Fuerza Motorizada"—an organic display of grassroots support.

Gerardo Leal was one of those organizers. By the time of the presidential election, his leadership and visible support for democratic change had made him a target.

This is his story.

July 2024 was hell.

Every day—threats. Every day—surveillance. Every day—alerts: "Don't go out today." "They're setting something up." "They're going to raid your house." At one point, I told my wife, "If something happens, don't run. Stay with the girls. Let them take me." Because if she ran, they'd take her too. And that fear—that daily fear—eats your soul. But I kept working. I kept organizing. I kept visiting people. Because the country needed us united.

Then came July 28, Election Day, the most dangerous day of my life. People inside the government—people I don't even know personally—would say, "Be careful—they're after your head."

My wife told me, "Don't go vote. They're going to arrest you."

I told her, "Don't worry. You go vote. I'll figure it out."

I sent her with a fellow *motorizado* for safety.

I didn't call anyone to avoid drawing attention. When I arrived at my voting center, everyone looked shocked: "What are you doing here?" People told me, "If you vote, you'll be arrested on the spot." Others said, "No—they won't arrest you. They'll kill you before you make it to the voting center."

I said, "If I don't vote, I'm already dead. If I vote, at least I die fighting." I said, "I came to vote, even if it's the last thing I do. I'm not betraying myself." The opposition people there supported me. The Chavistas knew me too—we're from the same neighborhoods. I said, "I trust the people here. They won't let anything happen to me."

They moved me to the front of the line—third person. I voted. Everyone was stunned.

As soon as I stepped outside, *colectivos*—armed progovernment groups—surrounded the block. Masked men. Motorcycles without plates. Someone came running toward me and said, "Gerardo—leave NOW. They're coming for you."

I left.

That was the last day I slept in my own house.

From that moment on, I went into hiding. I had nothing—just the clothes I was wearing and a small backpack.

I went to the mountains. I called a friend and said, "I need help." He said, "Come to my place, but be careful. They're looking for you everywhere." It was raining. Pouring. I was soaked. I was trembling from the cold and from fear. I got to his house, and he wasn't there. I waited outside. I didn't know what to do. I couldn't go back. I couldn't stay. A stranger—someone who lived nearby—saw me freezing and said, "Come inside, brother. Stay here." I didn't know him, but God puts angels in your path.

I slept there that night. That was my first night as a hunted man.

During that time, my wife lost everything. We had a business—a small shop. They took her out of it. They stole the merchandise. They seized everything. She couldn't work anymore. No one would sell to her because everyone knew what was happening. Everyone was afraid to be associated with us.

We ended up with nothing. Absolutely nothing.

*

I've been fighting the government for twenty-seven years.

I wasn't a politician. I was a *motorizado.* I was a humble worker dreaming of a better future. We *motorizados* know every street, every family. We took people around, helped with errands, and emergencies. And during protests, we were always there helping, guiding, and defending. That's why they targeted me, because *motorizados* can organize entire communities.

In 2019 the gasoline shortages were unbearable. We were waiting twenty-four, thirty-six, forty-eight hours and still not getting gasoline. So we decided to form the José Gregorio Hernández Motorcyclists Association—a *motorizado* guild—to stand up to the gas station owners.

The government didn't want us organized—because an organized people is strong. Every new military commander threatened to jail me.

*

In 2022 people started asking me to support María Corina. But I already had a big problem—they wanted to jail me over the gasoline issue.

Imagine if I went into politics then—they'd definitely arrest me.

I told my friend Guillermo, "They're going to screw me. They're going to jail me."

He said he'd defend me as a lawyer. Look where he is now—behind bars.

This isn't politics anymore—it's a dictatorship. I told people that many times. "This is a dictatorship."

And then came the 2023 primaries. I supported María Corina. I wanted to help. But I also had to think about my daughters and my wife. People were telling me, "Be careful. You're putting your family at risk. They're going to come after you harder."

If I went out on my motorcycle, two or three people would follow me. I'd turn, they'd turn. I'd stop, they'd stop.

And then the *colectivos* began sending messages: "Stay out of politics." "You don't know who you're dealing with." "You're next."

But I kept going because once you decide to fight, you can't turn back.

And I believed—and still believe—that María Corina represented hope. Real hope. Not political talk. Real change.

One day, a friend in the police—quietly—told me, "They already approved your arrest warrant. It can come down any day." I didn't sleep that night. I thought, *If they take me, at least let my family be safe.*

I prayed. A lot.

My family was scared. My daughters tried to be strong—but they're girls. They're young. My wife cried at night so I wouldn't hear. Sometimes I pretended to be asleep so she could cry freely.

We were living in fear. Pure fear. But at the same time, we were living with dignity. Because we weren't hiding what we believed.

But I couldn't stay quiet. The country needed us. The people needed us. I'd go house to house, talking to people, not campaigning for myself—I wasn't running for anything. I campaigned for *her*. She was the only one with the courage to face this regime head-on. My logic was simple: This wasn't politics anymore. This was survival. Every day the pressure got worse—especially on my wife. They would show up near the car. I couldn't stay at home. Every time I stayed home, someone would call me: "Leave. They're coming for you."

This is a regime of criminals. These people will hurt us.

Everywhere I went, people were desperate. They cried. They begged for help. And I carried all of that on my shoulders.

That's when I decided that I was going to give everything I have to this election. I didn't care if it cost me my freedom. I didn't care if it cost me my life. I just wanted my daughters to grow up in a normal country. Go to school. Study. Work. Live without fear.

Is that too much to ask? A normal life?

In Venezuela, yes—it's too much to ask.

*

On August 3, SEBIN arrived at my house. Not to take

me—because I wasn't there. They came to take my wife. My fifteen-year-old daughter was home. She saw everything. They forced the door. They grabbed my wife. They told her, "Call him. Tell him to come. If he comes, we'll release you. If he doesn't, you'll both stay detained." My daughter screamed, "Don't take my mom!" They put them in a truck. My wife with her hands shaking. My daughter crying uncontrollably.

They took them to intelligence police headquarters. My wife refused to call me. She told them, "If you want him, look for him yourselves. I won't help you catch him."

She's braver than anyone I've known. Stronger than me. They interrogated her. They yelled. They pressured her. My daughter heard everything from the hallway.

They let my daughter see her for a moment. My wife hugged her and said, "Don't be afraid. Your dad is alive. And he'll fight for us."

They held my wife for hours. Then they released her. But they told her, "If we don't find him in forty-eight hours, we'll come back for you. And next time, we'll take the girls too." That was the moment I knew I couldn't stay in Venezuela anymore. If I stayed, they'd destroy my whole family.

*

After everything, after seeing how they treated my wife, how they terrified my daughters, I made the decision: "I have to leave Venezuela"—not for me, but for them. So I told my wife, "I'm going to prepare everything. I'll find a way. And once I get out, I'll get you and the girls out too."

Getting out wasn't easy. Not at all. People warned me,

"Don't trust anyone. Don't talk on the phone." The route I had to take passed through dangerous areas—mountain passes, towns controlled by the regime. One wrong move, and they'd catch me. I had to disguise myself. Cover my face. Change clothes. Switch motorcycles. I rode with my head down. Avoided main roads. Went through back paths and dirt trails.

At every checkpoint, soldiers were stopping people. They had my picture in their hands. They were looking for me. I'm telling you—I trembled the entire trip. But God protected me.

The plan was to find a way to the Colombian border. But I couldn't let anyone know, not even friends and family, because if someone talked—even by accident—they'd catch me. I carried nothing but my ID, a little cash hidden in my sock, and faith. When I finally reached the border area, the fear multiplied. There were *colectivos* everywhere. Police everywhere. Checkpoints every kilometer. I had to pretend I was someone else. A mechanic. A delivery guy. Anything. I changed helmets. Changed jackets. Changed gloves.

And still—they looked at me like they recognized something. I prayed the whole way: "God, don't let them see my face. Don't let them stop me. Let me reach the other side."

When I finally crossed into Colombia, I cried. I'm not ashamed to say it. I cried like a child. I was shaking. Not from cold. From everything I had lived through. There, on the border, I cried again because it hit me: I had no country anymore. I had no home. I had nothing. But at least I was alive. And if I was alive, I could fight for my family.

That's all that mattered.

I didn't feel safe in Colombia. The *Tren de Aragua* was everywhere. Those criminals controlled entire neighborhoods. They charged protection money. They extorted Venezuelans. They killed people who refused to pay. The gang murdered someone three or four blocks from where we lived. We heard the gunshots. After that, my wife said, "We can't keep doing this. We can't die here." And it was true. We were risking our lives for pennies.

*

We had no legal documents. No right to work. No access to anything.

We lived month to month. Some days we ate well; some days we didn't. Sometimes friends helped—Venezuelans like us. Other times, we were completely alone. My daughters cried a lot. They missed their home, their room, their school, their friends. They couldn't understand why all this was happening. How do you explain dictatorship to a child? How do you explain hatred? How do you explain persecution?

All I could say was, "We're alive. And while we're alive, we keep going." Imagine reaching fifty-eight years old and having to start from nothing—like a newborn, but with the weight of an entire life behind you.

Then came the call from the UN. They asked about our case. They asked for our documents. They interviewed us. And they told us we were being considered for resettlement. At first, I didn't believe it. I thought it was a scam. I thought it was fake hope. But then the process advanced. They told us we had been accepted. They told us we were going to Canada. My wife cried. My daughters cried. I cried too. For the first time in a long time, we saw a light, a real light.

*

Coming to Canada—it feels like being born again. Everything is different. The language. The climate. The people. The customs.

Here, I have to learn everything again. How to work. How to speak. How to move. How to survive in a place that is safe—but completely new. Here, my daughters are safe. Here, my wife can sleep. Here, we don't jump every time a motorcycle passes.

Here, we are alive. But I'm not happy. I'm grateful. Happiness . . . happiness is in Venezuela. A Venezuelan is happy eating *hallacas* with family at Christmas. A Venezuelan is happy sitting around a table, talking, laughing. A Venezuelan is happy being with their people. Here, everyone works alone. Everyone is tired. Everyone goes to sleep early.

It's good—it's safe—but it's not home.

I want to believe the fight we gave was not in vain. I don't know if I'll live five years, one year, ten years. Only God knows. But I want to spend whatever time I have left in peace. Not running. Not hiding. Not looking over my shoulder. And I want my daughters to have what I didn't have: A future. A real future. That's why I don't regret anything, not one thing.

Everything I did, I did for them. For Venezuela. For a better country.

That's my story.

Meudy Osío

Fernando Albán was a councilman in Caracas and a member of the opposition party Primero Justicia. In October 2018, he was detained by SEBIN, Venezuela's intelligence service, after returning to the country from a trip abroad.

This is his wife Meudy's testimony.

I'm from Caracas. I'm a lawyer and a public accountant by profession. I was thirty-six years old. Fernando and I got married twenty-eight years ago—or, well, he would say thirty-six years ago, but for me, time stopped the day he passed away.

We were students when we met. We got married. We had two children—Fernando Alberto and María Fernanda. We had a very close family life; everyone who knew us can confirm that. Fernando was always involved in politics. We had an office in Venezuela where we provided services to different clients, both legal and accounting. We were always in Venezuela, in our office, working. Our lives were always centered around family—always involved in our church and in our community.

Even though Fernando was a politician, he used politics to help the people who needed it most.

In 2016 we started La Olla Solidaria (The Solidarity Cooking Pot) at Venezuela's Central University, in the university parish, where we served hot meals to about four hundred people every Sunday.

Our life was, as I said, very family-centered—focused on work, always attentive to our children. But in 2016, we had to take our children out of Venezuela because of everything that was happening—the threats.

We brought them to the United States so they could study.

I came in 2017, and Fernando was planning to come at the end of 2018, once he finished his term as a councilman for the Libertador municipality.

We had already decided that he would move here—our children were already studying, and we were adapting to life outside Venezuela. He had been meeting here with people from his party, opposed to the regime, and with some politicians who were in New York for the UN General Assembly meetings.

He went back to Venezuela to formally hand everything over—to leave everything organized—before joining us here for good.

Fernando returned to Venezuela on October 5, 2018. I never saw him again.

As a result of all the complaints we have filed, we have established that during those three days—from October 5 to October 8—Fernando's rights were violated: his right to defense, freedom from arbitrary detention, protection against enforced disappearance, freedom from torture, and his right to life.

He was held for more than twenty-four hours.

They allowed him to call me on Saturday.

He had been detained on Friday. On Sunday, he told me he was there. That's when we finally learned where he was—at SEBIN headquarters, the regime's intelligence service, on the tenth floor. They brought him before a tribunal, but there was no hearing that Sunday. On Monday, they were supposed to bring him again. They didn't. We didn't know anything. We had no information. That's when everything began. That's when we were told that he had supposedly "committed suicide"—that he had thrown himself from the tenth floor.

Then all the contradictions began—from the regime: that he had asked to go to the bathroom and jumped out the bathroom window, that maybe it wasn't the bathroom . . . all these contradictions.

To this day, we still don't know what really happened.

*

When I was told—when his political party's leader, Julio Borges, called me to tell me about Fernando's death—the first thing I said was: *They killed him.* Because our Catholic faith does not allow for that—and Fernando was not a man who would ever do such a thing. Never—not for a single moment—did I believe he could have taken his own life.

Our lives changed completely. For my children and for me—we were alone in another country, with no family, just the three of us. Fernando was always our pillar. He was always present, always involved—an active father, never a passive one. He was 100 percent engaged in everything related to our family. And it's not just me saying this as his wife—anyone who knew Fernando knows it is impossible to believe he committed suicide.

Even the cardinal at the time said it was impossible to believe.

*

The loneliness. Being alone here—the three of us together, yes—but without family, without the closeness of friends or relatives, we had to carry all of this on our own. I had to take the lead so my children could stay on their path—continue their studies, which was always our priority. And thank God, they did. My son is now a mechanical engineer. My daughter is a journalist.

We kept living—carrying the weight of the obligation to seek justice. We could not think, *It happened, Fernando died, and life moved on.* No—we are still searching for justice today. And that is the hardest part because justice feels further and further away.

Not just for him—for all those who have been killed, for all who have suffered injustice under that murderous regime.

*

I didn't know I was this strong. I didn't know I had so much conviction in the things I wanted to do. These contradictions in life either break you or make you stronger. Personally, I think I've been able to face an entire series of challenges—personally, publicly—speaking out, defending, and seeking justice. And I've tried not to be an example but to be a voice for many people who have suffered things even worse than what we've gone through and who don't have the platform I have because my husband was known—he belonged to a political party. But there are many anonymous people who've suffered the same or worse, and I have never spoken only for myself but always for all of us in this situation.

I know he watches over us. I always talk to him. I know he's with us. All the good things—and even the bad ones, which have become lessons—we've been able to carry because he's been with us. Even though he's not here physically, Fernando has always remained the same active father my children had and the devoted husband he always was. His teachings, his words—they've guided us. Always. Seven years have passed, but he's still here with us. My children have their own lives now—they're married—but we always come together, and his presence continues to unite us. It strengthens every decision we've made and every decision we will make.

*

We must believe.

We must keep hope alive—it cannot die.

Justice in Venezuela must come.

Freedom in Venezuela must come.

What we are living through is hard for everyone, though some suffer more than others. And right now, things have gotten even worse.

It's not just opposition politicians, not just journalists—now it's anyone who dares to say even the smallest word.

We must have faith.

We must keep hope alive for Venezuela's freedom, for our right to live in our own country, not to endure the hardships Venezuelan migrants face all over the world.

But we'll return to Venezuela, to a free Venezuela, full of opportunities.

I'm completely sure of that.

In May 2021, Venezuela's attorney general publicly stated that Fernando Albán did not die by suicide as initially reported but was killed while in SEBIN custody. Two SEBIN officers were later convicted in connection with his death, though those sentences were reduced, and both were released.

María Constanza Cipriani

In July 2024 Venezuela held presidential elections in which opposition candidate Edmundo González Urrutia received 67 percent of the vote. The National Electoral Council announced fabricated results and proclaimed Nicolás Maduro the winner. Following the election, the regime unleashed a massive wave of repression and detained opposition leaders, campaign staff, volunteers, and anyone connected to the elections.

On August 27, 2024, lawyer Perkins Rocha—María Corina Machado's attorney and the campaign's legal representative before the National Electoral Council—was detained in Caracas.

This is his wife María Constanza's testimony.

When I met Perkins, we were both legal advisors in different public institutions in Maracay, in Aragua state. He was an advisor to the State Legislative Council, and I worked as an advisor at the State Comptroller's Office. I'm a lawyer. We got married after a year and a few months of dating.

We have two sons: Santiago Andrés, thirty-one, an economist from Universidad Católica Andrés Bello, and Mariano Enrique, twenty-four, who just graduated as a video game designer from the University of South Wales in the United Kingdom.

Perkins is an only child, and like all only children, he tends to think he's the center of the world. But that same self-contained personality comes with an incredible kindness—a nobility of heart that defines him.

He doesn't hold grudges. He isn't vindictive. He forgets when people hurt him. Anger or resentment simply don't live in him. He's one of the kindest, most generous people I've ever known.

He's very studious—deeply devoted to law. He has two great passions: law and theater. When he was in college, he was a stage actor, and he still loves the theater passionately. He also loves music—classical music, heavy rock—he's eclectic. He hates commercial pop, unlike me. I love it.

He's a wonderful father—he leads by example. This situation has made me realize that all those family talks at the dinner table, when I never allowed a TV nearby, really mattered. In our house, dinner meant talking—or sitting in silence together—but never with a phone or device. Around that table, our sons learned respect and resilience. Right now, they're the ones saving me from losing my mind. In my darkest moments—and I have many—it's my sons who rescue me, saying, "Mom, calm down; this will pass."

That's been our dynamic—Perkins and I. We've always been a team. Even though we're both lawyers, we worked in different areas of law, so we complemented each other rather than overlapped.

I rarely asked him for legal advice, though, because he's meticulous, while I'm quick—I want fast answers. If I asked him a question, he'd give me a one-hour lecture. I'd say, "No, no—just tell me the conclusion!" and he'd reply, "No lecture, no answer." That was our rhythm—both at home and at work.

*

On August 27, 2024, everything changed. It had been one month since the regime stole the elections. Perkins already suspected he was being watched—and he was. I had gone back to Maracay for work; our law office is there. I had begged him not to go out until I returned because—childishly—I believed that if he went out with me, nothing would happen to him. I felt like Wonder Woman in those days.

But he went out because he needed to buy medicine for his mother, who lives in a nursing home in Caracas. He left the apartment—and they took him, either as he arrived at or left the drugstore. I still don't know exactly, because even though Farmatodo has many security cameras, we were never allowed to see the footage. But that was the location.

He went out to buy his mother's medication, and they abducted him.

I didn't see him again for fourteen months and eleven days.

I found out through my younger son—the one in the UK. Around 2:00 p.m., he called me. Perkins and I had been texting until about noon. I told him I needed to see some clients, and we'd continue later. That was our last conversation—I still have it saved.

At about 2:00 or 2:30 p.m., while I was with a client, my son called: "Mom, what's happening with Dad?"

I said, "Nothing, I just spoke to him at 11:30."

He said, "No—someone from Miami, one of my classmates, called to say Dad was taken—kidnapped."

I said, "No, impossible."

He said, "Mom, check."

I opened my phone and saw chaos on social media. I called Magalli, María Corina's campaign director, because I didn't know who else to call. "Maga, what's happening?"

She said, "We've been trying to reach you for an hour." She didn't know the details yet, only that they were making calls to find out.

Ten minutes later, she called again: "Yes, they took Perkins—apparently at Farmatodo."

I said, "I'm going to Caracas."

My brothers, who had also heard the rumor, came to Maracay, helped me pack, and drove with me to Caracas.

I immediately contacted a lawyer I knew. The next day began the *via crucis*—the torment—of going from one detention center to another, trying to find him. It didn't last long, because around 3:00 a.m., a public defender texted me saying she had assisted him in his initial hearing and that I should come in the morning to learn his place of detention.

When I went, she explained the supposed charges and claimed she had requested a conditional release—which I later learned was false. They never requested anything.

That was the start of the fight to free him—because the charges were absurd, based on two social-media posts from August 10.

One post was a reply to someone who wrote, "María Corina and the world want to set the country on fire."

Perkins responded, "That's a lie. We don't want to set the country on fire—we only want the truth to be respected."

The other was a photo of a young man hammering a statue of Hugo Chávez somewhere in Guárico state. Perkins said something like, "the town of"—I don't remember the name, maybe Zaraza—"also wants to be free." For those two comments, Perkins was arrested.

*

Fourteen months and eleven days.

Fourteen months and eleven days without seeing him.

We've been married for thirty-two years.

We were never one of those glued-together couples who did everything together. On the contrary, I think we've been able to withstand this because I don't have the sweetest temperament either, and we each had areas of our lives that were exclusively ours—where the other didn't enter. It was a way to preserve the essence that attracted us when we met: our independence.

I used to spend up to three months abroad with my sons sometimes, but we always had internet connection and saw each other a million times a day. To go from that familiar dynamic of having your partner present to suddenly not only not having him, but having him in that horrible condition—not seeing him, not speaking to him, not knowing how he was—it's a sensation I think I only managed to withstand without breaking because I said, "Okay, this is what it is. What do you have to do? Fight 24/7 to get him out."

For fifteen months, my life has been dedicated 24/7 to Perkins—completely.

No journalist can say they called me and I didn't answer. In the most absurd circumstances, journalists call me saying, "Can you record a video now?" and I'm somewhere looking like a crazy person, and I turn to whomever I'm with and ask, "Can you lend me your shirt?"

"Yes."

"And do you have some makeup?"

"Yes, I have some powder."

"Okay, put it here; I have to record a video."

My last fifteen months have been reduced to that—to

fighting nonstop for his freedom. And that's what has kept me focused. Even though I have dark moments, I keep the focus; I have an obligation. When they took him, I told my sons, "Don't worry—I'll handle it. I'll get him out." I owe my sons fifteen months. But fighting the regime is not easy. Still, every day I do my best to remain firm, for him, for getting him out. That is my commitment to my sons.

When I saw him for the first time in October, he was very thin. Very thin.

I am very particular—annoying, really. When I entered El Helicoide, at every checkpoint they asked, "Who are you visiting?" and I would answer, "Perkins Rocha, after fourteen months and eleven days."

At the next stop, "Perkins Rocha, after fourteen months and eleven days."

I repeated it all the way until I reached the visitation area.

They set a white plastic table for us—it looked dirty—and I said to the SEBIN officer, "Do I really have to sit here? Look, this looks dirty. I haven't seen my husband in so long; I think we deserve a nicer table."

He told me to choose any table I wanted.

I was choosing when the guard lifted his head. I turned, and there was Perkins.

I cannot describe the emotion I felt when I saw him after fourteen months and eleven days. I think that was the best hug of my life. He was very thin, but the hug was divine—so beautiful. I had longed for it so much. In that moment, I realized how little I had cried for him, because most of the time I had been focused: "I have to get him out. I have to get him out."

But in that moment, I allowed myself to be his wife again—not the hard woman fighting nonstop. I allowed myself to cry a little. When he tried to pull away, I said, "No, wait—don't pull me away yet. These tears are only for you. They can't see them. I haven't shed one tear in fourteen months and eleven days, and I won't let today be the day they see me cry."

After that, we sat and talked about everything—about our sons, about me, about what I do, about his incomprehensible daily routine in that place. In each cell he had to adjust to new companions and new habits.

He told me, "Now I understand your silences—you can't imagine how noisy it is. People coming into the cell, people who talk loudly or shout."

I used to complain that he would get up and turn on the TV, the iPad, the phone, the computer—and in each device he had a different news program. I would say, "No, I can't with all this noise. This isn't news—this is noise. I need a moment of silence when I wake up."

And that day he said, "You can't imagine how much I understand now how tormented you must have felt by my obsession with staying informed about everything." He told me something that moved me deeply: "In one of the cells, there is a tiny window where I can see the sky. I stand there in the mornings and pray the way you do at the apartment when you open your little window to pray."

It has been an extremely hard lesson for him. As an only child, he wasn't used to sharing—sharing spaces, sharing silences. It has been very complicated for him. He was always meticulous about his appearance—always neat, always pressing his white shirts.

*

I always say I'm not very good at giving messages. But I would say this: the first obligation of someone going through what I'm going through—what my family is going through—is to stay healthy.

I always start with that: you must stay healthy so you can truly support your loved one. And staying healthy means giving yourself moments to enjoy something you like—anything. And you must have a support network in your life, because we cannot do this alone. Alone, the burden is too heavy—especially living in Venezuela, where every day is a complication.

So we need that support network—whether family or friends—to help us carry the weight. And the focus must be on staying healthy, allowing yourself those small moments, and being tolerant and understanding with others. Because there are many people who want to give advice, and sometimes those pieces of advice become overwhelming.

So instead of going crazy from the overwhelm, take a deep breath and say, "Okay, focus."

After eighteen months in detention, Perkins Rocha was transferred to house arrest in February 2026. He remains confined at home under an electronic ankle monitor.

Elvira and José Gregorio Pernalete

In 2017 Venezuela experienced a massive wave of nationwide protests after the government moved to dissolve the opposition-controlled National Assembly and concentrate power. For four months, citizens marched demanding constitutional order and democratic restoration.

Security forces responded with sustained and militarized force. More than 120 people were killed during the protests.

Among them was Juan Pablo Pernalete, a twenty-year-old economics student and athlete, who was struck in the chest by a tear gas canister fired at close range by members of the National Guard. In the immediate aftermath, government officials denied responsibility and falsely claimed he had been killed by protesters. Independent forensic analysis later confirmed the cause of death.

This is the testimony of his parents, Elvira and José Gregorio Pernalete.

Elvira: We were two young people from very humble families. I'm from Guárico, and my husband is from Maracaibo, Zulia. We came to Caracas looking for opportunities. We married very young, in love, full of hope, wanting to work and struggle.

On December 1 of this year, we celebrated thirty years of marriage. We built a family. We dreamed of growing old together with grandchildren. We dreamed of being grandparents. I dreamed of retiring, of having a life where I could water plants, receive my grandchildren, and take care of my animals.

That was my dream. But our lives changed eight years ago—more than eight years ago—when we lost that illusion, that family we had dreamed of.

Being parents was central to the life project we were building as a couple.

Juan Pablo was born on December 28, 1996, at 8:30 a.m. When they placed him in my arms, I knew what happiness was. I knew joy. I knew my life had changed forever.

That was one of the most important things of our lives—being parents to Juan Pablo Pernalete and later to our daughter, María Gabriela Pernalete, whom we adopted in the following years.

We told him about the Venezuela we lived in. Even as a child, he asked why there was so much injustice, why children were eating out of the trash. After his death, we reread letters he wrote as a child. At thirteen years old, he wrote that whether we were Chavistas or opposition, we were all one country—that wars should end, that we shouldn't fight each other. Only after he died did we understand how much he carried inside.

José: We were a normal family. Like any other, we wanted a life plan to build toward day by day with effort and work. Everything revolved around our son, Juan Pablo. We placed all our attention on raising him, helping him move forward, making him into a good young man—someone who loved his country, who worked, who built a future. That is what anyone who longs for normality in a free country dreams of.

*

Elvira: Juan Pablo believed that protesting was not a crime. He believed that the country could change.

On April 26, 2017, we dropped him off at the university.

That day we were looking for medicines—there was severe scarcity. At noon he called me. We told him we were running late. He said not to worry, that he would go with friends.

That was the last time we spoke to him.

I received a call saying Juan Pablo was injured. I ran. I prayed. I begged God not to let them take him alive because I knew what they would do to him.

When I arrived, they told me, "You have to be strong. Your son is dead."

I found him. I tried to wake him up. He had an impact on his chest.

That moment was the beginning of hell.

*

José: From that moment on, they criminalized us. We were no longer parents of a victim—we were labeled parents of a "terrorist." They tried to destroy him morally after killing him physically.

Elvira: The authorities lied. From the first moment, they lied.

They said Juan Pablo had died because of a homemade weapon. Then they said it was a bolt. Then they said it was something else. But the truth is this: Juan Pablo was killed by a tear-gas canister fired directly at his chest by the Bolivarian National Guard.

That is documented. That is proven. But they tried to cover it up.

We made a decision: we would not remain silent. They tried to turn Juan Pablo into a criminal in the media. That's when we decided to fight for the truth. We didn't invent Juan Pablo's story. We simply told it.

From the very first moment, we realized that there was no intention to investigate the truth. The institutions were not there to protect us—they were there to protect the perpetrators. When we saw the lies, the manipulation of information, the attempts to blame Juan Pablo, we understood that no justice was to be found inside Venezuela.

That's when we decided to take the case beyond our borders.

José: We went to the Public Prosecutor's Office. We went to the Ombudsman's Office. We went to every institution that supposedly exists to defend human rights. And everywhere we went, doors were closed. They didn't want to investigate. They didn't want to hear us. They didn't want the truth. So we understood that this wasn't negligence—it was complicity.

Elvira: That's when we began to document everything. To collect evidence. To preserve testimonies. Because we knew that one day Venezuela would change, and when that day came, there would need to be proof.

*

Elvira: It has been exhausting, emotionally devastating.

Grief doesn't stop just because you're fighting. You're grieving while also having to be strong, to speak, to denounce, to relive everything over and over again. Every interview, every hearing, every statement reopens the wound.

But silence would be worse.

We've been followed. We've been threatened. We've been surveilled. We've received anonymous calls. Messages telling us to stay quiet. Warnings to stop talking.

But when you've already lost the most important thing in your life, fear changes.

José: You don't choose this path—it's imposed on you. We didn't want to become human rights defenders. We didn't want to become activists. We wanted to be parents. We wanted our son back.

Fear doesn't disappear—but it no longer paralyzes you. They already took our son. What else could they take from us?

That's when you understand that truth has to be spoken, no matter the cost.

*

Elvira: I don't forgive to free those who did this—I forgive to free myself because hatred destroys you from the inside. But forgiveness does not cancel justice. Justice must come.

José: We don't speak from revenge. We speak from truth and justice. Those responsible must be held accountable—not because we want vengeance but because a country cannot heal without justice. Without justice, wounds remain open.

Elvira: Juan Pablo was not a statistic. He was not collateral damage. He was not an accident. He was a young man with dreams, with values, with a future.

You don't get over the absence. You learn to live with it.

Pain doesn't fade. It transforms.

More than six years after Juan Pablo's death, charges were brought against National Guard personnel, but none have been effectively prosecuted or held to account within Venezuela's justice system.

Rafael Uzcátegui

In Venezuela's crisis, human rights defenders have been both chroniclers and casualties.

Rafael Uzcátegui spent seventeen years at PROVEA documenting state repression and supporting victims. As the government consolidated power, it systematically attacked those who exposed abuses.

After repeated public threats from senior officials and growing personal risk, Rafael left the country. His exile is part of a broader reality: the forced displacement of those who insisted on accountability.

This is his story.

I began working at PROVEA, the Venezuelan Human Rights Education Program, around 2006. I started in communications, later directed the research and information area, and eventually became general coordinator in 2015—until 2023. Nine years, three consecutive terms—the maximum allowed.

During that time, I gained a high public profile for two reasons.

First, through anarchism. I published a book in 2010—the first written from a leftist perspective critical of Chavismo. It's titled *Venezuela: The Revolution as Spectacle, an Anarchist Critique of the Bolivarian Government*. It was translated into English and French. That, along with my work in independent media, earned me enemies inside the government.

During the World Social Forum, the government organized in 2006, we held a parallel counterforum. And that sort of thing earns you enemies. The current minister of communication,

Freddy Ñáñez, is someone I knew then—and I know he's a personal enemy now. We all have a nemesis in the government.

Second, through PROVEA. I had to lead during difficult moments. In 2017, when mass protests erupted across the country, we were deeply involved in defending the right to peaceful protest. We documented state repression for international bodies, including the International Criminal Court. We also helped coordinate the visit of Michelle Bachelet—then the UN High Commissioner for Human Rights—whose 2019 report was unexpectedly strong and critical of the Venezuelan government, which had expected an ally.

Through all that, I was accumulating "debts" with the government for my activism. That's the path you choose.

I kept publishing. The Inter-American Commission on Human Rights issued protective measures for me. Within the Venezuelan human rights movement, I took a firm stance against authorities and pushed for unity within civil society.

I traveled several times to Peru, where I learned from colleagues who had defended human rights under Alberto Fujimori's dictatorship in the 1990s. One of the main lessons was that when democracy is at risk, the human rights movement must take a stand. In 2018 PROVEA officially classified Nicolás Maduro as a nondemocratic ruler—a dictator. For a human rights organization, that was a significant escalation. Given PROVEA's international prestige, it caused concern even among some allied groups.

I once had to prepare a report about my own situation of persecution. In the nine years I served as general coordinator, I received forty-one direct attacks from high-level officials—Tareck El Aissami, Diosdado Cabello (who targeted me the most), and at one point even Attorney General Tareck William Saab. There were also fifty-six indirect attacks: smear campaigns, defamation, and public criminalization.

We became a kind of "recurring trio" every Wednesday on *Con el Mazo Dando*—the state TV propaganda show hosted by Diosdado Cabello. They constantly featured Rocío San Miguel, Alfredo Romero, and me, accusing us of treason or of receiving foreign funding. They photographed us when we traveled abroad, claiming we returned with "dirty money."

*

At PROVEA I had a public role during very difficult times. Everyone was mobilizing, and that environment forces you to rise to the occasion. We worked hard to warn the region and our human rights colleagues about what was happening in Venezuela.

Not all efforts were effective, because many colleagues abroad—especially in leftist movements—had ideological sympathy for the Venezuelan government and refused to believe our reports. That was painful, because we shared the same theoretical values. If I came from Venezuela and told them something, they should have believed me more than Telesur or other proregime media.

That indifference hurt deeply. Still, we kept filing complaints and working with international organizations. Every time Diosdado Cabello mentioned me on television or said he would prosecute me, I had to leave my home. I developed a personal security protocol, which I followed strictly. You feel fear, but you try not to let it paralyze you. Having a support network helps.

After Rocío San Miguel's arrest, a contact inside the national identification agency warned me that my passport had been annulled and that I was on a list of people to be detained. That made me think seriously. I no longer had PROVEA's institutional shield. A volatile period was approaching—the 2024 presidential elections—and political prisoners were being openly used as bargaining chips in negotiations.

As repression intensified, those of us inside Venezuela had to be extremely careful. After consulting several international organizations that support human rights defenders, everyone advised that the most prudent decision was to leave the country—because of my public profile and the level of risk.

The minister of communication—my old nemesis—was openly hostile toward PROVEA and toward me personally. So I decided to leave. That was the hardest part. After so many years helping others—victims, families, people in need—I became someone who needed protection myself.

Defending human rights, for me, has meant a commitment not only to a cause but also, above all, to people—real people. We identify with a set of values; we've embraced the Universal Declaration of Human Rights and its principles. But what truly renews our commitment are the people we accompany—the people we learn from—who have gone through terrible, devastating experiences. And yet, despite everything, they remain joyful, they don't lose their will to live, they still long for justice, and they persist despite threats.

That is deeply instructive. It constantly reminds us of the beauty and resilience of Venezuelans. As long as victims exist, we have a personal and moral commitment to them.

Leaving Venezuela was very hard. I told myself, *I'm going to continue helping from wherever I am.*

Human rights work has helped me grow as a person. Anarchism, though iconoclastic, is also part of the broader left—and it carries its own sectarianism and arrogance. Human rights work has made me more tolerant, more open. My identity as a human rights defender now stands above everything else. I've learned to recognize the right of others to be different from me, to think differently, to disagree.

And it's also a challenge—because tomorrow, in the transition we hope and fight for, we will have to defend today's victimizers. If they are detained and denied due process, we will have to defend them—just as human rights organizations defended Hugo Chávez during the April 2002 coup attempt—a failed military uprising in which Chávez was briefly removed from power.

That's a real challenge, because we are human—we feel anger. But that is the vocation we chose. We are preparing to defend those who once oppressed us—not to allow impunity, but to ensure that justice is done properly.

*

Seeing myself as an exile, as a forced migrant, even as a victim, was very hard. I needed therapy to work through migratory grief. My father had died two months earlier. The uprooting, and especially the guilt that all social leaders feel when they leave, was very heavy. You feel terrible at first, especially when you learn that friends or colleagues are being detained.

Now I'm trying to see being in Mexico City as an opportunity—to learn, to help Venezuela from another place, to keep a voice. The hardest part is being far from Venezuela, far from people who need support at this moment. But it's also true that those inside have fewer and fewer tools to work with.

Maybe life placed new challenges in front of me, and I'm trying to face them. Nostalgia, not knowing when you'll see loved ones again, and the uncertainty of returning to your country—that's very hard.

My wife and I bought an apartment in Venezuela—our first real home—and we only spent two Christmases there. She also works in human rights. Even though she had a lower profile, she was involved in things that required caution. I try not to think about our home because it's painful. What I miss is not an abstract idea of a nation—it's places and people where I was happy.

*

This may sound contradictory, but my father was very Chavista until he died. Before that, he had been a member of Acción Democrática, the traditional social democratic party that dominated Venezuelan politics for decades. When Chavismo came, he saw hope. He watched state television all day. He and I spoke very little about politics. We respected that boundary because we knew we didn't agree at all.

That helped me as a person and a sociologist to understand Chavismo as a political phenomenon and from that understanding to try to confront it. Some politicians have done that partially, but what I hope for the country is this: I'm sure we will get out of this sooner or later. Chavismo is in its terminal phase. That phase may last weeks or years, but its golden age is over. Losing popular support is decisive.

Understanding the expectations people had, explaining them, and working from there is essential. Venezuela was a country that fell in love, then became disillusioned, and is now trying to fall in love again. Many see in María Corina Machado someone who can lead them to a new romance. It's important to understand what she represents politically, but more importantly, to understand what people feel—their expectations.

I've learned to understand people—to understand a country as particular as Venezuela—and to work with real human beings. We hope for perfect leaders or perfect activists, but what we have is what we have, and we must work with that—build a country with the luminousness and the dark we all have.

I've learned that we are a country with tremendous opportunities and immense human quality. And maybe we have searched in others—in savior figures—for what we already have. Hopefully, the great lesson is this: yes, we need leadership, but that leadership is a reflection of who we are. I hope we learn from these thirty years so we don't repeat the mistakes that brought us here. That's my greatest fear—not that Chavismo won't end, because it will, but that we haven't learned enough not to repeat the errors that led us to this situation.

We will recover from this. We will come out of this as a country. We just have to find inspiration in each other.

Danieli Gabriela Hernández Sánchez

On August 26, 2024, following the presidential elections, Nélida Sánchez—national coordinator of training for Súmate—was detained by SEBIN officers in Los Teques. Súmate is a Venezuelan civil organization founded in 2002 to promote electoral participation, citizen oversight, and the defense of political rights; its leadership has faced criminal proceedings over its work and has been repeatedly targeted by state actions.

Nélida is also a former longtime employee of Venezuela's National Electoral Council (CNE)—the same electoral authority that fabricated the 2024 results and has refused to publish disaggregated vote tallies to this day. In the run-up to the election, she oversaw the training of more than 100,000 polling station monitors across the country to help safeguard the vote. Her work was central to the historic efforts by civil society to support electoral integrity and prove the regime's fraud.

This is her daughter Danieli's testimony.

On August 26, 2024, I was in the United States, in Seattle, visiting my aunt—my mother's only sister.

That morning, during one of our usual calls to Venezuela—we're four hours apart—we video-called my grandmother. She was sitting in the passenger seat of her car, accompanied by two women, one of whom was driving. Her tone and expression told us something was wrong.

We asked who she was with. At first, she said they were neighbors helping her with errands. That was strange—my grandmother never lets anyone use her car.

As soon as we hung up, I called my mom. When she didn't

answer, I told my aunt, "Call Grandma again. Mom has been taken."

We called again. She was still in the car with those two women. We asked directly: "Are you with SEBIN or not?"

She said yes.

And from that moment on, everything descended into chaos.

I had texted with my mom barely two hours earlier on WhatsApp. The feeling that follows is indescribable—you don't know what to do or what comes next. The only thing you feel is fear—a lot of fear.

*

I'm thirty-two years old. I'm a twin; we were born on November 22, 1992. We always lived with my mom. I lived with her until July 26, 2024, when I had to leave Caracas. I left the country to set up a technical command center in Bogotá in support of the July 28 election. I never came back.

My childhood was very calm. We spent most of our time with my grandparents because my mom worked a lot. She worked for twenty-seven years at the National Electoral Council, Venezuela's official electoral authority. She was a single mother. During election periods—there were so many elections in those years—she worked nonstop, so after school we stayed with my grandparents.

I'm a lawyer like my mom, who's a certified public accountant and a lawyer. When I began studying law at the Central University of Venezuela in 2010, she began her law degree at Universidad Bicentenaria de Aragua. We graduated the same year—my ceremony was a few months earlier because her university is private—but we received our degrees basically together.

After I graduated, I began working at Súmate, where she worked as well.

My mom is someone who loves her work. She truly loves what she does. She entered the CNE because my grandfather had been the regional director of the Miranda state office—he was her boss. She joined because of him, and then she built her career there.

My mom has always been extremely passionate about her work. She gives everything she can so that things turn out well. At the time, I didn't see it clearly, but now I understand her dedication and commitment—not just at the CNE but also at Súmate. My mom is a deeply committed woman, to the point where she's in the situation she is now.

She is a woman who gives herself completely, who, when she believes in something, does not stop until she fulfills it.

At first, when Hugo Chávez came into power in 1999, she believed there could be a social—not economic—change for Venezuela. But along the way, everything turned out as it did. But my mom never voted. She didn't vote because she worked in the electoral body. She avoided voting unless there were municipal elections, because those are for your own community. But she always avoided anything that could raise questions.

In the 2024 election, she played the same role she has had since the 2017 elections. She is the National Coordinator of Training for the NGO. The organization, since its foundation, has worked for years supporting political organizations with electoral processes, both technologically and through training.

My mom is the person who designs and structures the voting manuals, coordinates how training will be carried out, decides which states will receive trainers, and organizes the national trainer pool—the team that travels locally to train polling station members, election staff, and electoral witnesses, or *testigos*.

She decides which topics are included in training sessions and oversees evaluations to ensure people understand the material and are committed. She leads all of that with her team.

My mom worked up until the day I left the country, because *testigo* credentials were submitted until July 25–26. She had also been coordinating the citizen oversight team.

After July 26 she focused on monitoring the elections process, helping gather information for our press department and providing legal basis for publications we could have issued. But she didn't have operational work after that. In my case, I was more involved, but she wasn't.

*

There was a time—after she was arrested—when my mother was allowed to call me. Now she can't make international calls. The few times I speak with her—maybe a couple of minutes a week—are when she calls my grandmother from El Helicoide prison on a regular phone line. My grandmother then calls me on WhatsApp, and we do a three-way relay so I can hear her.

My grandmother and my sister are still in Venezuela and have access to her—they can visit twice a week.

Her health is our biggest concern. Just yesterday, she had another hypertensive crisis that required treatment in the medical area of El Helicoide. She has been waiting four months for surgery to remove veins in her legs because she has chronic vascular deficiency. She had a similar surgery eight or nine years ago.

She has been on psychiatric medication for four or five months. She was diagnosed and medicated inside El Helicoide around May of this year. She started having symptoms of PTSD and moderate depression.

She also developed night terrors after a raid in her cell at the end of last year. Since that raid, she has had severe PTSD symptoms.

She has fibromyalgia and already suffered at least one documented crisis requiring additional medication.

She only sees the sun two days a week—for thirty minutes. She is in a windowless cell with four other women, sharing one bathroom.

She tries to stay strong, and we try to do the same.

*

I think the hardest part for me is the deprivation of maternal affection.

I lived and worked with my mom for thirty years, until I had to leave Venezuela. After leaving, I had one month when we could speak daily. After that, it has been almost total silence.

Yes, it becomes part of a new routine—fifteen months have passed—but I never get used to it. I still dream about her freedom. I've had hundreds of dreams imagining how she'll walk out, how we'll reunite.

I would trade places with her without hesitation. Any day.

Beyond exile and starting a new life elsewhere, the hardest thing is not having my mom—her not knowing my day-to-day life. I haven't been able to tell her about the incredible people I've met or the ones I hoped to never see again.

She missed my sister's medical graduation. She missed her specialization graduation.

She has missed two years of birthdays—for all of us.

We have a little cousin turning five now—she has missed the last two years of his life—almost half his life.

My grandfather has dementia—he's ninety-four. My mom was one of the few people he still recognized and spoke to. After fifteen months without seeing her, he forgot her too.

My mom was the one who supported my grandmother in everything. My aunt has been outside the country for eight years. I would say, without a doubt, that after the pain I've felt, my grandmother is the one who has suffered the most. She witnessed her daughter's arrest—she was with her that day.

She has had to be incredibly strong. I hope this ends soon so she can rest.

*

I think—among many lessons, because there isn't just one—the most valuable is realizing that sometimes we don't appreciate what we have. We chase things that aren't truly valuable.

If you ask me what I would give to be with my mom again, I'd tell you that I'd give everything.

When something so essential is taken from you—your family, your home—and you can't do anything to recover it—

We've done everything legally possible inside and outside

Venezuela. But the biggest lesson is that material things don't matter. We get attached to them, but they aren't important. They really aren't.

No matter what we believe in, we must always keep faith. Everything happens for a reason. Even if it's painful—even if the lesson is forced and hurts—eventually we understand why we had to go through it.

As a family, we remind ourselves every day that we have learned to love each other more through this process.

So that would be my message: trust, keep going, keep fighting, stay steady, and wait. Everything will pass.

And one day we'll look back and understand why we needed to go through it.

Nélida Sánchez was released from detention on February 10, 2026, after being held for over seventeen months.

Ramón Guanipa

In the aftermath of Venezuela's July 28, 2024, presidential elections, a new wave of repression targeted opposition leaders, campaign staff, and activists. Among those affected was Juan Pablo Guanipa—a leading opposition politician, former governor-elect of Zulia State, vice president of the National Assembly for Primero Justicia, and a prominent ally of María Corina Machado—who was forced into hiding and later detained in Caracas.

This is his eldest son Ramón's testimony.

In the months leading up to the election, it was my father and I managing the house, taking care of the kids, getting them ready for school. We had lost my mother only a few months before. We were getting used to a new routine while grieving my mom's passing, and at the same time my dad continued in the final campaign push before the election.

So we were living through our own family process, and he still hadn't taken his foot off the accelerator as a politician.

Then, the July 28 elections come. He leaves, he votes in our home state of Zulia and goes to Caracas. Being the eldest, I had asked him, "Dad, what's the plan? Should we expect things to reach certain points? Should we expect a turbulent day? Could anything happen?"

And the last thing he said to me was, "*Chamo*, I'm going there to give my life if necessary."

That meant he expected to return but knew he might not. I just digested what he said without reacting. I understood that was the plan, and that was the commitment.

So he left.

July 28 came, and he didn't return.

The wave of repression by the regime began—the new wave—and he was forced to go into hiding, into protection. That hiding started to extend—it went from weeks to months. And we reached a point where we thought, "Okay, this is until this ends." Or as María Corina says, "This is until the end."

Months passed. We had, in a surreal way, gotten used to it. As Venezuelans, we develop adaptation skills to stressful, abnormal situations unique to us. We adapted to everything being online, to being at a distance. My dad would tell me what to do with the household, what needed to be done. I handled getting the kids ready for school and running my own life. I'm twenty-nine, I have a daughter myself; we're five siblings and one granddaughter—so everyone was in the same house, and he was online.

(When I say "online," I mean through calls or encrypted messages—he stayed in communication with us while in hiding, coordinating everything remotely.)

*

I don't live in Caracas, where he's being held, but I have family there. The routine is that I bring him lunch to prison and every day ask the guards about him. Every day, I ask what he needs. Many times they say he doesn't need anything; other times they say, "Bring books, bring medicine." They say they will take care of things. So we're always there, always knocking on the door. From a distance, I am always asking my relatives, insisting.

My dad spent ten months in hiding and has been in prison

for seven. My younger siblings and his granddaughter haven't seen him in over a year and a half. I've only been allowed to visit him once—they let me see him for twenty minutes. It's the first and only time I was able to see him in person after all that time—a visit fully recorded and supervised. And after that, no more visits.

The first thing he told me after greeting me—and he said this in front of the policemen, with a camera on the table—was "I'm not going to walk out of here like those who leave thanking them or aligning themselves with the regime. They won't get that from me. I will always stay strong and firm in what we are doing and in the struggle we are leading."

He told me that while wearing a blue jumpsuit, visibly emotional.

The visit was short. We mostly talked about the kids, about things at home. Even from prison he's thinking about the house—how the kids are doing at school. Two of them are about to graduate from high school. He's keeping track of everything, delegating tasks to me.

That shows not only the politician he is but also the father he is. A man in prison is thinking about his children's school as if that were more important than his own safety. And for him, it is.

So I want to insist that we remain proud and deeply honored to be his children, and we carry this with dignity.

The day-to-day becomes uncertainty. Every day is one more day for him. He's about to reach seven months. Seven months go by quickly when you say it, but when you're in prison, they're not quick. All we hear is "He's fine. He's fine. He's fine. He doesn't need anything. He's fine." But I don't know how he is health-wise. I don't know if physically or mentally he's well. I don't know if he has lost weight or gained weight. We know nothing beyond what a guard might say.

*

At the same time, I have to try to take care of everything at home—the kids. I try to create a pseudo-normality in this situation. Uncertainty is the most important factor in this problem. You can adapt to many things—to routines, to methods. What you can't adapt to is uncertainty—not knowing what will happen tomorrow.

Not knowing if tomorrow there will be a sham trial, or a sudden sentence, or a health emergency that no one can treat. You don't know.

So you dissociate. You bury yourself in routine—school, work, university, errands, even getting gas. Everyday tasks fill your mind so you can cope. But every now and then, you stop and think coldly, *When will he get out? When will this end?*

We don't count on the regime's goodwill—we don't expect it. We haven't been timid in calling them what they are: a criminal narco-dictatorship that persecutes people for anything, that checks your phone at a checkpoint, and can imprison you over a few words.

Our only hope is that this regime falls and that freedom brings the release of political prisoners.

Not seeing him is hard—especially at Christmas. The children already spent one Christmas without their mother and with their father in hiding. Now it's another Christmas without their mother and with their father in prison.

They are all old enough to understand what's going on, but I still try to ease their pain, and mine. That's what's hardest.

He is missing graduations, birthdays, soccer games, learning-to-drive conversations—all the ordinary things that matter most. I'm a father myself, so I know what that means. We are losing time with him, and that's one of the hardest blows a family can take.

*

If there's something I can take from this entire process, it's that when you face hardships—and I'll paraphrase Viktor Frankl here—when you face moments where you feel you've reached the limit, the only thing you have left is your will, your dignity, and your honor.

My father is the symbol of all that. He has always known that his life was at risk. This isn't the first time he's been targeted.

In 2017 he won the governorship of Zulia, one of Venezuela's most important and productive states. It's a position that could set you up for a comfortable life if that's what you're looking for in politics. Instead, he treated that office as a trench from which to increase pressure against the regime. Everything he has done, everything he has sacrificed, has been to end the dictatorship.

And he showed it the day he said he would not kneel. All he had to do was swear allegiance before Maduro's Constituent Assembly—just shake his hand. Some would say it's courtesy, some would say it means nothing.

And because he refused a handshake, my father was removed

from office, persecuted by state intelligence. We were harassed for two years after that decision.

And even then, he held on to his principles.

Dignity is just that: what lets you look in the mirror without looking away. And my father has taught me they cannot take our dignity unless we let them.

My dad never softened his discourse, never surrendered. We all knew the struggle he was leading would have consequences. And we knew July 28 was probably the most important day in our history. It was a presidential election when we had everything against us—and we won. We finally slammed our fists on the table. So we knew they wouldn't let that stand.

This is the price of fighting for freedom. This is the price of fighting for democracy. It's not cheap. It's not paid in cash. It's paid with dignity, sometimes with blood, with pain. This struggle has cost people their lives.

So when you fight for freedom, you give everything. And that is our case. My father has given everything. And I want to highlight that far from being sad or resentful, we are profoundly proud of him.

In February 2026, Juan Pablo Guanipa was released from prison and was shortly thereafter taken into custody again. The following day, he was transferred to house arrest and later granted full freedom. He has since resumed political activity and continues to advocate for the release of all political prisoners.

Rubén González

The Guayana region in southeastern Venezuela is home to the country's so-called basic industries—the iron, steel, and heavy industrial complexes that for decades formed the backbone of national production and employment.

For years, Rubén González led union efforts at Ferrominera Orinoco, one of Venezuela's largest state-owned iron companies. His case became emblematic of the crackdown on independent labor organizing under Hugo Chávez and later Nicolás Maduro, as unions were pressured to align politically with the government.

This is his testimony.

The real problems began in the 2000s, when Chávez took control of the industries and began politicizing everything. From that moment on, everything changed. Chávez wanted the unions kneeling. He wanted the workers kneeling. He didn't want a worker with dignity—he wanted submissive workers. And I was never submissive. Never. I told him so publicly, more than once.

I was born on March 17, 1959. At seventeen, I left home looking for work. I settled in southeastern Venezuela and worked at SIDOR—Siderúrgica del Orinoco, the state-owned steel company—for two years. After that, I found work at Ferrominera Orinoco—the state-owned mining company. I started there in 1984, first in the Pellets Plant—in the warehouse—receiving, storing, and distributing material. That's where I learned the basics.

From there, I got involved in the union movement. The workers needed someone who would defend them, and I've always been a fighter. I began attending assemblies, participating in meetings. Little by little, I took on more responsibility, until I became secretary of the union.

I always told the *compañeros*, "The most important thing a unionist must have is dignity. A unionist is not a boss, not a slave. A unionist is a servant—a servant of the workers. And a servant must listen, must be attentive, must be responsible."

That's the foundation—not politics. Service.

*

The first big confrontation came in 2008. We were defending the collective contract. The government wanted to impose clauses that harmed the workers, and we said no—firmly and democratically. They sent the National Guard against us. They used tear gas, shields, and batons. But we didn't move.

One officer told me, "González, don't stand in front. They're going to shoot."

And I answered, "If I don't stand in front, the workers lose."

The example must come from the leader. If the leader hides, the workers won't fight. That fight ended with a victory—we defended our contract. But we also ended up on the government's blacklist. From that moment on, they marked me.

In 2009 the persecution became open. We held another peaceful march. The National Guard blocked the road and charged at us—without warning. Tear gas, rubber bullets, beatings. They attacked older workers and women. And then they blamed me. They accused me of "instigating violence." Me—a man who always defended peaceful protest.

They issued an arrest warrant. I was detained, taken to prison for marching, for defending workers' rights—for doing what the constitution guarantees. Seventeen months. Seventeen months unjustly imprisoned.

Prison marks you. You see the cruelty of the system. You see what power does to a man without God. But God sustained me. Inside, I prayed, read scripture, and encouraged others.

After seventeen months, they released me provisionally.

*

The case was sent to Caracas, and I spent five years on trial. Five years going to hearings, five years facing prosecutors, five years facing a justice system that was completely corrupted. I faced all of them—all their "witnesses," all their lies, not because I was stronger than anyone but because I had no crime to confess.

I was freed on March 3, 2011. In the end, they declared me innocent of all charges.

*

Throughout those years, I kept working at Ferrominera Orinoco, representing the workers. Even while on trial, I organized stoppages—because conditions were terrible. No tools, no safety equipment, no uniforms, no boots, no gloves. The machinery was broken, the cranes failed, the belts didn't move. Everything was falling apart. And the government didn't care.

The regime destroyed the industry intentionally. They wanted workers dependent on the state, kneeling for crumbs.

Wages were miserable. Benefits and bonuses were eliminated. And those who protested were persecuted.

*

The persecution didn't stop—not even for a day. In 2011, 2012, 2013—every time we protested, every time we demanded food, health care, safety equipment, or contract rights—they threatened me again. And then, in 2018, they imprisoned me a second time.

We were protesting because the regime had eliminated the collective contract. We fought because what they did was unconstitutional—they violated the rights of all workers. And once again, they blamed me. They said I was "inciting hatred," "instigating rebellion," "engaging in sabotage," and all those false accusations the regime uses. They came for me like I was a criminal.

They took me straight to La Pica, a maximum-security prison—without investigation, without trial, without any legal process. From one moment to the next, I was locked up again. And let me tell you something: La Pica is not a normal prison. La Pica is hell. It's full of very dangerous people. That's where they put me—a union leader, a man who never carried a weapon, a man whose only "crime" was demanding that the government follow the collective contract.

The ones I feared were not the prisoners—it was the officials, because officials follow orders. And the orders were "Break González." "Isolate him." "Wear him down." But I stayed calm. I stayed firm. And I put everything in God's hands.

The officials denied me medical attention many times. They

refused to take me to the infirmary. They told me to "resist." They told me to "hold on." Imagine that—treating a sick, innocent man like that.

My family suffered terribly too. My wife had to travel hours and hours to bring me food. The conditions were degrading. And outside, the persecution against my family continued. That's the cruelty of this regime—they don't just imprison you, they punish everyone around you.

There were moments when I felt exhausted, when I felt my body couldn't take any more. But every time I reached that point, God lifted me. Every single time.

And besides God, there was something else: my conscience. I always said to myself, *Rubén, you did nothing wrong. You defended the workers. You defended the truth. You don't owe them fear.* When a man knows he's innocent, he finds strength. When a man knows his cause is just, he finds courage. And when your fight is for others—not for yourself—you don't break.

The hardest moment was when my grandchildren asked me, "*Abuelo*, why are you in prison?" It broke me. But I told them the truth: "Because I defended the workers. Because I refused to lie. Because I didn't kneel." And they hugged me. And that hug gave me more strength than anything else.

Another very hard moment was seeing my wife arrive for visitation—tired, hungry, carrying food she bought with sacrifice. I saw her stand in line under the sun for hours just to see me for fifteen minutes. That hurt me more than prison itself. A man can endure prison—but seeing his family suffer is the real torture.

At one point, they transferred me to Monagas state for a

supposed hearing—a "trial." They kept postponing it, month after month. A legal farce. Justice doesn't exist under this regime. My family protested outside. Workers from all over Guayana demanded my freedom. International organizations pressured them. And finally—after twenty-eight months—they released me. But they never cleared my name. Never. They know I'm innocent, but they don't care.

Twenty-eight months. Twenty-eight months in that hell. Twenty-eight months of injustice. Twenty-eight months of humiliation. Twenty-eight months away from my home, from my family, from my work.

It was hard coming home after those months—very hard. Emotionally, spiritually, physically—everything. Prison breaks you. And when you come home, you're not the same man. You're marked. You carry the fear, the memories, the injustice.

*

The intention was clear: they wanted to break the backbone of the workers' movement.

But we resisted. Even with hunger, even with threats, we resisted. Meetings in secret. Assemblies in the streets. Conversations at dawn. Workers whispering about their problems because they were afraid the intelligence services were listening.

Everything had to be done quietly, carefully, with courage. And the government criminalized even that. Any gathering was labeled "conspiracy." Any complaint was "instigating hatred." Any protest was "terrorism." Imagine that—a worker demanding his salary being labeled a terrorist.

That is the absurdity we lived through.

But we didn't stop. Despite the fear, despite everything, the workers of Guayana remained firm. And that's what the regime couldn't stand. They want silence. They want obedience. They want submission. But the workers of Guayana have dignity, and that's something they could never erase.

*

What do I dream of now? What do I want for Venezuela?

Freedom. Justice. Dignity. I want a Venezuela where no one is imprisoned for speaking the truth. Where workers have rights, not crumbs. Where industries are strong again. Where families don't have to be separated—children in one country, parents in another.

I want the industries of Guayana restored. They are the heart of Venezuela. They gave food, education, and opportunity to tens of thousands of families. Seeing them destroyed breaks my soul. I want to see them alive again, full of workers, full of production, full of hope. One day—with God—we will see that again.

I love my country. I was born in Venezuela. I fought in Venezuela. I suffered in Venezuela. And I raised my family in Venezuela. Why should I be the one to leave? Let the criminals leave. Let the ones who destroyed the country be the ones to run.

Not me.

I have learned that one man—even alone—can resist a dictatorship. Not by force, not by weapons, but through dignity and faith. I learned that suffering shapes you. That pain refines you. That injustice teaches you what true justice should look like. I learned that a man without convictions is like a tree without roots—it falls with the first wind. But a man rooted in God . . . that man cannot be moved.

People need to understand that what happened to me is not an isolated case. I wasn't the only one they persecuted. Many workers suffered what I suffered—some even worse.

There are workers who were beaten, who were tortured, who were disappeared. Workers who were fired unjustly, who lost everything, who went into depression, who ended up begging.

I don't carry resentment. I carry memory. I've forgiven those who persecuted me, because forgiveness frees the soul. But forgiving doesn't mean forgetting. Forgetting injustice is dangerous—forgetting allows it to repeat itself. I forgave the men who carried out the orders, but I won't justify the evil of those who gave the orders. Justice must come—but justice, not revenge.

Rubén González was pardoned and released in September 2020. He remains active in labor advocacy, calling for the freedom of jailed workers and the restoration of workers' rights in Venezuela.

Magalli Meda

A few months before the 2024 presidential elections, Venezuelan authorities issued arrest warrants against several senior members of María Corina Machado's campaign team, including her campaign manager, Magalli Meda. She and five other colleagues entered the Argentine Embassy in Caracas to seek protection from detention.

For over four hundred days, they remained inside the diplomatic compound as Venezuelan security forces maintained a continuous and heavily armed presence outside the premises. During that period, the embassy experienced extended interruptions of water and electricity service.

In May 2025 the group left the embassy in a coordinated extraction and departed the country.

This is Magalli's story.

On March 20, 2024, arrest warrants were issued for eight members of María Corina's senior campaign team and political leadership. Henry Alviárez, chief of organization, and Dignora Hernández, political secretary, were intercepted and imprisoned that morning. That same day, I entered the Argentine Embassy in Caracas, along with five of my colleagues. I would spend the next fourteen months there under asylum.

Inside were Claudia Macero, head of communications; Pedro Urruchurtu, head of international relations; Humberto Villalobos, elections chief; Omar González, political secretary; and Fernando Martínez Mottola, political advisor to the opposition coalition. From within a diplomatic compound under permanent armed surveillance, I directed a presidential campaign that won 67 percent of the vote against the regime—using the very tools and data the regime itself had created to execute its fraud.

The campaign manager for Nicolás Maduro was Jorge Rodríguez. The campaign manager for Edmundo González Urrutia—the opposing side—was me. He was free; I was trapped, isolated inside an empty embassy.

When the Argentine diplomatic mission was expelled from Venezuela, the embassy remained for twenty-four hours without a flag. For twenty-four hours, there was no diplomatic protection. We understood how exposed we were. Brazil later assumed external representation, but from outside the compound. No diplomatic mission approached the premises after that. In the final month of our confinement, the International Committee of the Red Cross was the only institution permitted to enter.

The regime's security forces cut the water, the electricity—everything—and even stripped the electrical fuses, leaving us that way for six months. Not a drop ran through the pipes. We relied on unfiltered reserves drawn from the bottom of the tanks. Illnesses became routine—mouth infections, skin conditions, episodes of fainting. There were days when one of us would collapse, and the rest would improvise care. Even under those conditions, we divided responsibilities and continued working. Electoral strategy sessions took place in the dark. Communications were drafted without electricity, and we managed to charge our phones sparingly through a single fan fitted with a small solar panel. We were enduring confinement while building a national campaign.

Fernando was allowed to return home through a negotiated

arrangement. Not long afterward, he died. The siege stole his health.

After the July 28 elections, the perimeter tightened further. The regime confiscated three adjacent properties along the northern side of the embassy compound and expelled their residents. Marino Mendoza, an embassy employee who had worked there for years and who brought us food under supervision, was jailed and held for over a year. An Argentine gendarme was also arrested amid escalating tensions.

We eventually escaped in secret and had to flee the country to save our lives. But the retaliation did not stop there. Diosdado Cabello, Maduro's enforcer and currently interior minister, wanted to hurt me. So he began targeting my family.

My mother—seventy-nine years old—had to flee Venezuela with my child. My husband, Jorge Olavarría, refused to leave me alone while I remained under asylum and went into hiding instead. Even after our escape, the pressure did not stop.

My family lost everything. Everything. They took my house—my home, where my children and husband lived. They went to my mother's house and took everything. Inside my mother's house—where the memories of my family were—they took everything and set up a command post inside.

When I say they took everything, I mean they didn't leave a single pair of pants. Diosdado even has my medical exams, my children's photos, my father's memories.

I don't like to play the victim—it's not just me. But it shows the magnitude of a criminal model advancing over everything, without even pretending to keep up appearances.

*

María Corina began traveling across the country in support of Edmundo. The repression during the campaign was horrific—truly horrific. Wherever we went, restaurants where we stopped to eat were shut down. Hotels where we slept were inspected, fined, and in many cases closed. Families in towns where we stayed were arrested. They would take the relatives of the hosts to jail. The cars we parked were burned.

The regime began to imprison our campaign staff. They kidnapped four of our regional campaign directors: Emil Brandt Ulloa, campaign director for Barinas; Guillermo López, campaign director for Trujillo; Juan Freites, campaign director for Vargas; and Luis Camacaro, campaign director for Yaracuy. They are all still kidnapped today.

So when I say it was a campaign of persecution and repression, I mean brutal persecution. And yet, because people saw María Corina was willing to move forward despite persecution, Venezuelans felt it was their responsibility to join. People joined massively.

No road she traveled lacked hundreds of people waiting to greet her. No town she stopped in lacked crowds telling her, "We're with you." It became a social movement unlike anything in Venezuelan history.

*

I began getting involved in this political fight in 2010. I received an invitation to a meeting where María Corina was forming a team to run for a congressional seat. I went to that meeting, and she had a lot of doubts—she had never done politics.

I had spent my career in television production, communications, and design. I had never been involved in politics. But I'm a strategic person—and I had a very clear sense of what a campaign needs.

She immediately connected with me and asked if I could help her for a few months. I offered her three months of work in 2010—almost sixteen years have passed, and I'm still here.

It became . . . a slightly extended project. The reason is that this is a cause that affects all of us as a nation. I understood clearly that if we weren't part of the solution, then we were being part of the problem. And it has been many years of learning alongside to María Corina. I directed her 2010 congressional campaign, where she won the most votes of any legislative candidate in history. After that, we decided to build a political party—Vente Venezuela. What began as a short project became a lifelong commitment.

*

That's how we arrived at the 2023 opposition presidential primaries—perhaps the most important milestone to understand the moment Venezuela is living today and the real opportunity for change.

On October 22, 2023, manual primaries were held as a citizen-led effort. Across the territory, Venezuelans protected the process. People stayed at the voting centers and ensured that the vote count reflected the truth. After twenty-six years, we finally had an electoral process where people could see the truth with their own eyes.

María Corina won with 92 percent of the vote. By that night, the campaign had evolved into a national unity movement called Con Venezuela.

It was no longer about María Corina—it was about Venezuela. That became the force that brought together political organizations willing to move forward united toward the possibility of dismantling a criminal model. It was beautiful—and a huge learning moment for the political parties too. A powerful coalition emerged of all the noncaptured political parties, independent leaders, and citizens across the country.

The regime, in response, disqualified María Corina—declared she couldn't run. Everyone expected her to say, "Okay, this is as far as we go."

Instead, a national unity team immediately began searching for a person who could represent the dignity of a country and who would not negotiate their victory. That's how Professor Corina Yoris emerged—an older woman, an academic, chosen to represent what the regime called the "placeholder candidate." She accepted—and immediately, the regime disqualified her too.

Then came a long process until Edmundo González Urrutia was allowed to register as a candidate. The regime needed a counterpart—even while repressing, persecuting, imprisoning, killing people—they needed a face for the other side. Edmundo was allowed to register because they had a plan: he would later be replaced by a candidate convenient for the regime, someone who would hand over the victory to Nicolás Maduro. But Edmundo acted like a warrior. He resisted the pressure. He stayed on the ballot.

And that's how we reached July 28 with Edmundo González Urrutia as the candidate.

*

María Corina is a woman with enormous courage. She's not doing this for herself, because she's not the candidate. When we finally declared it would be Edmundo, she presented him to the country with her popularity sky high, holding a poster with his name and face. She told the country, "Vote for this man." And the people said, "We will do whatever you say." And that's how Edmundo González Urrutia won.

And remember, Venezuelans abroad were not allowed to vote. Young people who were eligible to vote were not allowed to register. Anyone who had just reached voting age was blocked—they didn't allow them to sign up.

And even with that, Edmundo González Urrutia became the legitimate president of Venezuela with 67 percent, with teams working in hiding, with María Corina enduring persecution, with her whole team exiled, hidden, imprisoned, tortured, or killed.

She carried out a heroic campaign so that Edmundo González Urrutia could represent national sovereignty. And in that process, we built a project—a project designed to deploy a structure of six hundred thousand Venezuelans defending the vote.

There are thousands of stories—antennas hidden in houses, scanners smuggled around, people doing their part: the woman who held the *acta*, the person who delivered food, the one who used her ironing board to count votes because there was no table, the motorcycle courier who secretly transported *actas* to be transcribed. Everyone played a part.

This was something we built together. And that's why the country feels this process is theirs—and why they've decided to defend it even with their lives.

We have more than 890 political prisoners today. From our campaign alone, more than 290 people are still kidnapped. The list is overwhelming—high-profile people still kidnapped, not for days but for fifteen, eighteen, twenty months, in the worst prisons in Venezuela, just for doing their work in the electoral process.

So yes, my personal sacrifice was enormous. We lost everything. But I am just a tiny example compared to thousands across the country and abroad who lost the most sacred things: their families, their homes, their property, their lives.

My work has always been in service of building citizenship in politics—being part of the solution and the reconstruction of democracy. I never imagined that doing so would cost my family everything. But if defending the truth of an election demands sacrifice, then that sacrifice is part of the responsibility we assume when we choose freedom.

Since leaving the Argentine Embassy in May 2025, Magalli Meda has continued her role in exile as a senior strategist for María Corina Machado's political movement. She has moved seven times in nine months.

Edmundo González Urrutia

In October 2023, Venezuela's democratic opposition held presidential primaries in which María Corina Machado won an overwhelming majority of the vote. The Maduro regime subsequently banned her from running in the 2024 presidential election.

Facing a narrowing space and severe repression, the opposition coalition selected career diplomat Edmundo González Urrutia as its candidate. Despite unequal conditions and escalating intimidation, the July 28, 2024, election produced an overwhelming victory for Edmundo.

The official authorities declared Nicolás Maduro the winner and refused to publish disaggregated results. What followed was a renewed wave of arrests, forced disappearances, and political persecution targeting campaign staff, electoral volunteers, and members of González's family.

This is his testimony.

My name is Edmundo González Urrutia. I am Venezuelan, born in La Victoria, in the state of Aragua. Thanks to the support of the Venezuelan state, I was able to pursue a career in international relations, even though my father initially believed that profession was not meant for people from a middle-class background like ours.

I devoted my entire professional life—just over three decades—to the foreign service, until my retirement a few years ago. Among the most significant postings where I had the opportunity to serve were El Salvador, Algeria, and Argentina, all of them during periods of deep political conflict. In those years, I worked in countries experiencing civil wars or abrupt changes of government, which marked my understanding of public service and responsibility.

Although I served the Venezuelan state, most of my career fortunately took place during years of democratic governments, before the so-called Bolivarian Revolution began at the start of the twenty-first century. I never felt affinity with that political project and disagreed with it from the outset. For that reason, I chose to request my retirement.

The foreign service is a very particular profession. One is called to defend and project the image of one's country before the international community. I did not feel comfortable, serious, or responsible representing a regime with which I felt no connection—quite the opposite. I preferred to retire rather than continue in that role.

That decision forced me into early retirement, with eight to ten years of service still ahead of me. It naturally entailed both personal and financial losses.

The most difficult moment, however, did not come with my departure from the diplomatic service but with the situation Venezuela faced in 2024. Despite María Corina Machado having won the October 2023 primaries by a wide margin, the regime unjustly disqualified her from running in the presidential elections the following year.

The democratic forces were then confronted with the need to find a candidate who could keep alive the hope of an electoral victory and who would also be allowed to compete. After complex negotiations, and under considerable pressure from the regime, the opposition parties agreed that my candidacy was the most viable option.

It was not an easy decision for me. We knew that accepting

the candidacy would change our lives completely. After discussing it as a family, we decided to take that step, because when the country calls, one cannot turn away.

What followed is well known: a campaign throughout the country under very difficult conditions, an extraordinary level of popular organization, a decisive victory with more than 67 percent of the vote, and later, persecution and exile here in Madrid. Since then, nothing has been easy. But the decision we made was necessary, and without question, we would make it again.

The gravest consequences of this process have fallen on my family. My son-in-law, Rafael Tudares, who had never participated in politics, was abducted at the beginning of 2025 while taking my two grandchildren to school. They were left alone on the street as their father was taken away.

More than eleven months later, we have still not been allowed to see him, nor has he been permitted access to his lawyer. Despite the absence of any evidence that he committed a crime, he was recently sentenced to thirty years in prison. And like him, there are many innocent people who are being subjected to serious violations of their fundamental rights.

If there is one lesson I have learned through these circumstances, it is the importance of remaining faithful to oneself and of defending what we value most in life. One never knows what fate may bring, but if we remain true to who we are and to what we believe in, life ultimately calls on us to give our best. Many things in life come down to honesty, patience, and perseverance.

To those who will read this testimony, I say the following: if we stand firmly in defense of the values and principles with which we were raised and if we share a democratic vision for our country, those convictions will not disappear easily. The roots that anchor us in democratic values are Venezuela's strongest foundation to rebuild itself and once again become the vibrant democracy it once was, admired by many nations.

Rafael Tudares was released from detention in 2026 following sustained national and international pressure. No credible evidence was ever presented to substantiate the charges against him.

NOBEL PEACE PRIZE SPEECH BY MARÍA CORINA MACHADO

Introduced and Delivered by Ana Corina Sosa Machado
December 10, 2025

Good afternoon.

First, I want to express our infinite gratitude—from my family and from an entire country—to the Norwegian Nobel Committee.

Thanks to you, the struggle of an entire people for truth, freedom, democracy, and peace is today recognized around the world.

I am here on behalf of my mother, María Corina Machado, who has united millions of Venezuelans in an extraordinary effort that you, our hosts, have honored with the Nobel Peace Prize.

But although she has not been able to be here to take part in this solemn ceremony, I must say that my mother never breaks a promise.

And that is why, with all the joy in my heart, I can tell you that in just a few hours we will be able to embrace her here in Oslo, after sixteen months living in hiding.

As I await the moment to hug her, I think of the other daughters and sons who do not get to see their mothers today.

This is what drives her. What drives all of us. She wants only to live in a free Venezuela, and she will never give up on that purpose.

That is why we all know she will very soon be back in our country.

In the meantime, at this moment, I face the difficult task of giving voice to her words—the speech she prepared for this occasion.

This is her speech.

*

Your Majesties, Your Royal Highnesses, distinguished members of the Norwegian Nobel Committee, citizens of the world, my dear Venezuelans:

I have come here to tell you a story: the story of a people and their long march toward freedom.

This march brings me here today as one voice among millions of Venezuelans who rose, once again, to reclaim the destiny that was always theirs.

Venezuela was born of audacity, shaped by peoples and cultures intertwined. From Spain we inherited a language, a culture, and a faith that merged with ancestral Indigenous and African roots.

In 1811 we wrote the first constitution in the Spanish-speaking world, one of the earliest republican constitutions on

Earth, affirming the radical idea that every human being carries a sovereign dignity. This constitution enshrined citizenship, individual rights, religious liberty, and separation of powers.

Our ancestors carried liberty on their backs. They crossed an entire continent, from the banks of the Orinoco to the heights of the Potosí, to help give rise to societies of free and equal citizens, out of the conviction that freedom is never whole unless it is shared.

From the beginning, we believed something simple and immense: that all human beings are born to be free. That conviction became our national soul.

In the twentieth century, the earth opened: in 1922 the Reventón in La Rosa erupted for nine days, a fountain of oil and possibility.

In peace, we turned that sudden wealth into an engine for knowledge and imagination.

Through the ingenuity of our scientists, we eradicated disease. We built universities of global prestige, museums and concert halls, sent thousands of young Venezuelans abroad through scholarships, trusting that free minds would return as transformation. Our cities glowed with the kinetic art of Cruz-Diez and Soto.

We forged steel, aluminum, and hydropower—proof that Venezuela could build anything it dared to envision.

Venezuela also became a refuge.

We opened our arms to migrants and exiles from every corner of the earth: Spaniards fleeing civil war; Italians and Portuguese escaping poverty and dictatorship; Jews after the Holocaust; Chileans, Argentinians, and Uruguayans escaping military regimes; Cubans escaping communism; and families from Colombia, Lebanon and Syria seeking peace.

We gave them homes, schools, safety. And they became Venezuelans.

This is Venezuela.

We built a democracy that became the most stable in Latin America, and freedom unfolded as a creative force.

But even the strongest democracy weakens when its citizens forget that freedom is not something we wait for but something we become.

It is a deliberate, personal choice, and the sum of those choices forms the civic ethos that must be renewed every day.

The concentration of oil revenues in the State created perverse incentives: it gave the government immense power over society which turned into privilege, patronage, and corruption.

My generation was born in a vibrant democracy, and we took it for granted. We assumed freedom was as permanent as the air we breathed. We cherished our rights, but we forgot our duties.

I was raised by a father whose life's work—building, creating, serving—taught me that loving this country meant assuming responsibility for its future.

By the time we recognized how fragile our institutions had become, a man who had once led a military coup to overthrow the democracy was elected president. Many thought charisma could substitute the rule of law.

From 1999 onward, the regime dismantled our democracy, violating the Constitution, falsifying our history, corrupting the military, purging independent judges, censoring the press, manipulating elections, persecuting dissent, and ravaging our extraordinary biodiversity.

Oil wealth was not used to uplift but to bind.

Washing machines and refrigerators were handed out on national television to families living on dirt floors, not as progress but as spectacle.

Apartments meant for social housing were handed to a select few as conditional rewards for obedience.

And then came the ruin:

Obscene corruption; historic looting. During the regime's rule, Venezuela received more oil revenue than in the previous century combined. And it was all stolen.

Oil money became a tool to purchase loyalty abroad while at home criminal and international terrorist groups fused themselves to the state.

The economy collapsed by more than 80 percent.

Poverty surpassed 86 percent.

Nine million Venezuelans were forced to flee.

These are not statistics; they are open wounds.

Meanwhile, something deeper and more corrosive took place. It was a deliberate method to divide society by ideology, by race, by origin, by ways of life, pushing Venezuelans to distrust one another, to silence one another, to see enemies in one another. They smothered us, they took us prisoners, they killed us, they forced us into exile.

It had been almost three decades of fighting against a brutal dictatorship.

And we had tried everything: dialogues betrayed; protests of millions crushed; elections perverted.

Hope collapsed entirely, and belief in any kind of future became impossible. The idea of change seemed either naive or crazy. Impossible.

Yet, from the very depths of that despair, a step that seemed modest, almost procedural, unleashed a force that changed the course of our history.

We decided, against all odds, to run a primary election, an unlikely act of rebellion. We chose to trust the people.

To rediscover one another, we traveled by road and by dirt path in a country with gasoline shortages, daily blackouts, and collapsing communications.

Forbidden from advertising, without money or media willing to speak our names, we crossed it armed only with conviction.

Word of mouth was our network of hope, and it spread faster than any campaign, because our desire for freedom was very much alive within us.

The forced migration that was meant to fracture us instead united us around one sacred purpose: to reunite our families in our land. Grandparents confided in me their greatest fear: dying before meeting their grandchildren abroad; little girls, with voices too small for such sorrow, begged me to bring back their mothers and siblings scattered across continents.

Our pain fused into one heartbeat: bring our children home, now.

In May 2023, during a rally in the small town of Nirgua, a teacher named Carmen came up to me. She told me she had just run into her Jefa de Calle—a regime agent assigned to Carmen's block who decides, house by house, who receives a monthly food bag and who is punished with hunger.

Shocked to see this woman there, Carmen had asked her, "Why are you here?"

The Jefa de Calle replied, "My only son, who fled to Peru,

asked me to be here today. He told me that if you win, he will return home. Tell me what I have to do."

That day, love defeated fear.

Two weeks later, we reached Delicias, a tiny village swallowed by Colombian guerrillas and drug traffickers, where not even a chicken can be sold without criminal permission. No candidate had gone there since 1978.

As we climbed the mountain, I saw Venezuelan flags waving from every humble home. I naively asked if it was a national holiday. Someone whispered, "No. Here the flag stays hidden. Bringing it out is dangerous. Today people raised it to thank you for daring to come. You will leave . . . but we will remain, identified."

Entire families stood up to the armed groups that ruled their lives. And when we sang the national anthem together, sovereignty returned in a single, fragile, defiant chorus.

That day, courage defeated oppression.

Our gatherings became intimate encounters of thousands.

We embraced, we cried, we prayed.

We understood our struggle was much more than electoral.

It was ethical—the struggle for truth.

Existential—the struggle for life. Spiritual—the struggle for good.

With less than a year before the presidential election, we had to unite every democratic force and restore trust in the vote. The primaries became that moment: a self-organized civic effort that built a nationwide citizen network unlike anything Venezuela had ever seen.

On October 22, 2023, against all odds, Venezuela awoke.

The diaspora, a third of our nation, reclaimed its right to vote.

The son who left cast his ballot alongside the mother who stayed.

Lines stretched for blocks. Turnout was so overwhelming that ballots ran out. We trusted the people, and they trusted us back.

What began as a mechanism to legitimize leadership became the rebirth of a nation's confidence in itself. That day, I received a mandate: a responsibility that transcended any individual ambition. I felt humbled and profoundly aware of the weight with which I had been entrusted.

Threatened by that truth, the regime prohibited me from running for president. It was a harsh blow, but mandates belong to the people.

So we set out to find another candidate who could take my place.

Edmundo González Urrutia stepped forward—a calm, brave former diplomat. The regime believed he posed no threat.

They underestimated the resolve of millions of citizens—a plural, vibrant society that, in all its diversity, found unity in a common purpose. Communities, political parties, unions, students, and civil society stood together and worked as one so that the voice of a nation could be heard.

We were three months from Election Day, and almost no one knew his name.

But votes were not enough; we had to defend them. For over a year, we had been building the infrastructure to do so:

Six hundred thousand volunteers across thirty thousand polling stations, apps to scan QR codes, digital platforms, diaspora call centers. We deployed scanners, Starlink antennas, and laptops hidden inside fruit trucks to the furthest corners of Venezuela. Technology became a tool for freedom.

Secret training sessions were held at dawn in church backrooms, kitchens, and basements, using printed materials moved across Venezuela like contraband.

Finally, Election Day arrived on July 28, 2024. Before dawn, lines wrapped around blocks. A quiet, trembling hope filled the air. Our live tracking showed turnout rising across every state and town. And then the electoral tally sheets—the famous *actas*, the sacred proof of the people's will—began to appear, first by phone, then WhatsApp, then photographed, then scanned, and finally carried by hand, by mule, even by canoe.

They arrived from everywhere, an eruption of truth, because thousands of citizens risked their freedom to protect them.

Confronted with our overwhelming victory, the regime issued a desperate order: soldiers were to expel our volunteers from voting centers and block them from receiving the original tally sheets they were legally entitled to.

But the soldiers disobeyed.

Edmundo González won with 67 percent of the vote, in every state, city, village.

Every single tally sheet told the same story.

Within hours, they were digitized and published on a website for the world to see.

The dictatorship responded with terror.

Two thousand five hundred people kidnapped, disappeared, tortured.

Homes marked.

Entire families taken as hostages.

Priests, teachers, nurses, students, anyone who shared a tally sheet, hunted down.

These are crimes against humanity, documented by the United Nations. State terrorism, deployed to bury the will of the people.

Some of the more than 220 children detained after the elections were electrocuted, beaten, and suffocated until they repeated the lie the regime needed, falsely incriminating themselves of being paid by me to protest. Women and girls in prison are right now being forced into sexual slavery, made to endure abuse in exchange for a family visit, a meal, or the chance to bathe.

And yet, the Venezuelan people did not surrender.

During these past sixteen months in clandestinity, we have built new networks of civic pressure and disciplined disobedience, preparing for Venezuela's orderly transition to democracy.

That is how we reach this day, a day carrying the echo of millions who stand at the threshold of freedom.

This prize carries profound meaning; it reminds the world that democracy is essential to peace.

And more than anything, what we Venezuelans can offer the world is the lesson forged through this long and difficult journey: that to have democracy, we must be willing to fight for freedom.

And freedom is a choice that must be renewed each day, measured by our willingness and our courage to defend it.

For this reason, the cause of Venezuela transcends our borders. A people who choose freedom contribute not only to themselves, but to humanity.

We attain freedom only when we refuse to turn our backs on ourselves; when we confront the truth directly, no matter how painful; when love for what truly matters in life gives us the strength to persevere and to prevail.

Only through that inner alignment—that vital integrity—do we rise to meet our destiny. Only then do we become who we truly are, able to live a life worthy of being lived.

Along this march to freedom, we gained profound certainties of the soul—truths that have given our lives a deeper meaning and prepared us to build a great future in peace.

Therefore, peace is ultimately an act of love.

This love has already set our future in motion.

Venezuela will breathe again.

We will open prison doors and watch thousands who were unjustly detained step into the warm sun, embraced at last by those who never stopped fighting for them.

We will see grandmothers settle children on their laps to tell them stories not of distant forefathers but of their own parents' courage.

We will see our students debate ideas passionately and without fear, their voices rising freely at last.

We will hug again. Fall in love again. Hear our streets fill with laughter and music.

All the simple joys the world takes for granted will be ours.

My dear Venezuelans, the world has marveled at what we have achieved. And soon it will witness one of the most moving sights of our time: our loved ones coming home—and I will stand again on the Simón Bolívar bridge, where I once cried among the thousands who were leaving, and welcome them back into the luminous life that awaits us.

Because in the end, our journey towards freedom has always lived inside us.

We are returning to ourselves. We are returning home.

Allow me to honor the heroes of this journey:

Our political prisoners, the persecuted, their families, and all who defend human rights; those who sheltered us, fed us, and risked everything to protect us; the journalists who refused silence; the artists who carried our voice; my exceptional team, my mentors, my fellow political and social activists; the leaders around the world who joined and defended our cause; my three children, my adored father, my mother, my three sisters, my brave and loving husband, who've all supported me throughout my life; and above all, the millions of anonymous Venezuelans who risked their homes, their families, and their lives out of love.

To them belongs this honor.

To them belongs this day.

To them belongs the future.

Thank you.

POSTSCRIPT

On January 3, 2026, Nicolás Maduro and Cilia Flores were captured in Caracas during a US military operation and transferred to the United States to face federal charges, including narcoterrorism and drug trafficking. Maduro has appeared in the US District Court for the Southern District of New York, where criminal proceedings are ongoing.

In the months since, some—but not all—political prisoners in Venezuela have been released, and efforts to restructure the country's energy sector have involved US participation. María Corina Machado has emerged as a prominent voice in international discussions about Venezuela's future governance, meeting with world leaders and advocating for the release of political prisoners and an elections timeline.

ACKNOWLEDGMENTS

This book, in itself, is an acknowledgment—to the mothers of Venezuela, to the Venezuelan people, and to the courage, resilience, and love that have kept hope alive in our nation.

It was made possible thanks to the dedication and generosity of Emiliana D., Ivann M., Miguel Ángel M., and the team at Skyhorse Publishing, including President and Publisher Tony Lyons, Hector Carosso, Jon Arlan, Adam Szetela, and Brian Peterson.